How Women Manipulate:
Essays Toward Gynology

By

David C. Morrow

Copyright © 2004 by David C. Morrow

ISBN 0-7414-2058-9

Published by:

INFINITY
PUBLISHING.COM

1094 New Dehaven Street
Suite 100
West Conshohocken, PA 19428-2713
Info@buybooksontheweb.com
www.buybooksontheweb.com
Toll-free (877) BUY BOOK
Local Phone (610) 941-9999
Fax (610) 941-9959

Printed in the United States of America
Printed on Recycled Paper
Published May 2004

Contents

Preface

These essays, written over about twenty-five years, appeared (with a couple of exceptions) in such men's rights publications as *Transitions* and *Aladdin's Window* as well as journals with a wider scope, *Critique* for example. My main purpose has been to enable men to overcome their lifelong training in deifying and mystifying women and become able to criticize and evaluate them as human beings. The social institutions that support and enforce false beliefs regarding women, including the courts, the media, chivalry, and feminism are a barrier to men's self-development and also come under analysis. The final end of this is the objective study of women, which I call *gynology*.

I owe much to persons who offered advice and who have been willing to publish these essays despite general antagonism to the notion of men as complete persons rather than tools and workhorses for women and the state. An admittedly incomplete list would be Bob Banner, publisher of the much missed *Critique*, F. Baumli, editor of *Men Freeing Men*, R. F. Doyle, publisher of *The Liberator,* J. R. Molloy, who published *Aladdin's Window*, Rod Von Mechelen of *Backlash*, and Tom Williamson of *Transitions*.

What We Have Here is a Failure to Cooperate

It is women, of course, who can't commit. They just wait till marriage puts them in control of a man's property and income before copping out, which is the real reason half of all marriages end in divorce and most of the plaintiffs are women. Nearly every marriage is now a power struggle between self-centered females and husbands working to build a family; because government created and maintains the situation, women almost always succeed in divorcing or in destroying the meaning and fulfillment of marriage.

Because men have begun to realize this and opt for other arrangements or for singleness, women bitterly accuse them of lacking commitment. Because men have begun to figure out women's manipulation techniques, they have raised the shrill chorus of accusations that have helped ramrod "wife rape" and other legislation against which there is little defense. Yet men's constructiveness and desire for natural family life still lead most to marriage.

And there are cases where divorce is less likely. Some women take their religious beliefs seriously enough to be above rationalizing their own trespasses. Others, with few outside prospects, have husbands who don't make enough money for it to be profitable. A wise husband may protect himself with a premarital contract, and there are a few men whom women see as ideal. Divorce is nevertheless a possibility in these and similar situations because it has become so thoroughly a part of our culture that it offers women rewards beyond the financial. If it did not, and if it were as painful as they claim it is, they'd avoid it despite the money and certainly never keep repeating the experience.

Divorce earns women high status among females. Women admire and envy divorcees as they entertain them with tales of degradation, sex, and unbearable martyrdom followed by vindictive triumph, rehearsing useful accusations and alibis. Women compare and evaluate legal maneuvers, manipulative strategies, and the characters of men and of women not present ("sharing feelings" in Femspeak) and lose no opportunity to do so with someone of proven success. Basking in female attention and envy, the divorcee finds a perverse meaning in her experience, feeling herself to be living out a grand drama more exciting and more important than the mundane chores of responsible living, seeing herself as victim, soldier, spy, victor, martyr, moralist, and teacher.

Through divorce a woman gains a lifelong enemy and scapegoat, a permanent excuse for everything wrong in her life, and a legally approved victim for perpetual emotional and financial abuse. The ex --- usually the first in particular --- husband caused all her problems and brought on all her failures; he damaged her so badly the effects persist forever. He is always hurting her even if he lives a continent away and never makes contact, or he is neglecting his responsibilities even if he lives nearby, pays support and insurance and bills, visits the kids per schedule, and never intrudes. He's secretly trying to get her to perform the unspeakable acts he forced on her during marriage...

The ex-husband is quite useful in dating. His hideous depravity and mistreatment of her explain any *faux pas* the divorcee commits. She can use him to control subsequent companions through rivalry; many, if not most, will compete with the image she presents. They will work at being better behaved or at living up to her version of the ex's wealth and the scant good qualities she allots him. She will probably try to make her dates hate and fear the ex (no matter what he's really like) and might even have them physically attack him, a relatively safe action since as a matter of course *he* will be assigned the legal and social blame.

Custody of the ex-husband's children, a virtual certainty, is rewarding beyond its economic benefits. However, the father's presence can show up her lies about him and irritate new partners when it isn't useful to the divorcee, while despite women's freedom to use and abuse men's children, he actually can offer them some protection. Accordingly, the divorcee's goal is almost always to destroy the father's relationship with his children while continuing to plunder his income. The methods used by ex-wives to achieve this are familiar to most of us and provide a clear example of the female tactical mind.

She will usually try to discourage him, an easy strategy, made easier by the fact that confrontation is always seen as oppression of the woman. When he picks up the kids, the divorcee throws tantrums, screaming and weeping as she indicts him for all her troubles and pretends to have all manner of anxiety about his

2

taking "her" kids. A woman may act as though inarticulate with grief, or may alternate politeness with rage, sentiment with threatening body language. The divorcee will often muster friends and relatives to be present as an intimidating cadre whenever the father must see her, or have her boyfriend or new husband join in, perhaps in a good cop/bad cop intimidation routine. Whenever the boyfriend is around, the divorcee makes sure the kids call him "dad" and that he gives them money and gifts the father, stuck with supporting both his ex and himself, can't afford.

The children are tools in this, and also the second strategy. The divorcee uses body language, verbal subtleties and staged scenes when she "doesn't realize" the kids are witnesses to undermine their respect for their father and make them fear and resent, if not hate, him. She will give him false information about the children's routines, needs, and interests, or none at all, and "forget" to supply academic and medical records. Once this is done she will tell him, angrily or politely, sometime in pretended pain, that he has treated them all wrong, even when he's done exactly what she said to, telling him further lies about how he has harmed everyone, pleading with him to cooperate. She often interferes with visitation, usually by "legitimate" means; for example, she may plan a trip to Disneyland during scheduled visitation, leaving the father to miss his time with his children, or play the grinch.

If she can't alienate the father or drive him to violence, the divorcee will try to hide from him. She will move repeatedly without giving him her address. She will go to another state, if possible the furthest one there is, or to another country. Since her ex pays visitation costs, this will probably eliminate him. If it doesn't, she may take the kids to various doctors and send them to many art, dance, music, and sports classes, and send him the bills; or charge him with sexual abuse. The divorcee justifies her relocations on the basis of her own and subsequent partners' jobs (and the kids' needs for treatment and education), then she can explain the father's attempts to maintain a relationship as "stalking" her or as lust for the children. If he takes legal action because of any of the maneuvers described above, the father has to pay her legal fees as well as his own, and in addition he has to pay court costs even in those rare cases where he wins the lawsuit.

3

These examples of female manipulative strategies also show another function of custody, which is to provide women with drama and excitement. They are a source of fun because they can be used to hurt the father and his family. They are relatively helpless individuals whom the divorcee can control and use, at least till they grow up and become equally gratifying examples of callous ingratitude. Children are a link to other women and a means of displaying one's self-sacrifice to the world. Further uses of children in divorce are discussed in "Toward Gynology," *Aladdin's Window* # 12. [See page 51 of this volume.]

Destroying the father's relationship with his kids, ruining him financially and socially (her hostility and rage are directly proportional to the banality and falsehood of her divorce pretext -- - and the court's crookedness) are a main source of fun for vengeful ex-wives. Divorce also enables women to live out their sexual fantasies as well as the power trips women never really separate from them. The divorcee again becomes (as before her marriage) the center of male attention, surrounded by men to pick and choose among. Although she'll most likely select her next husband for financial reasons, she may for the first time in her life refrain from appraising the economic value of each and every suitor, since her ex (and often the government) supports her now --- and she may have a job to provide additional income. Nevertheless, further partners will usually pay her way on dates, fix her car, do chores she can't (or won't) and pick up the tab for sundry expenses as they vie for her favors.

Divorce as we know it is a major factor in making personal and ethical maturity unnecessary for women. That their almost inevitable success has nothing to do with their personal qualities or any necessary connection with femaleness doesn't keep it from inflating their egos. Women's immaturity, augmented by androphobic propaganda, lets them believe each time that they have won a great victory against men and oppression, and that their court mandated support by others is independence. Avoiding the hard work of growing up, they have --- like spoiled brats --- the leisure and incentive to cultivate skills of manipulation.

Yet there are men who are not readily deceived or divorced by women. For reasons considered in "No Secrets" (*Aladdin's Window* # 11) [see page 7 of this volume], women's ideal mate isn't simply powerful (or at least rich), but preferably a foreigner. He should be emotionally troubled and addicted to alcohol (if not cocaine), or perhaps some benign illegal substance like pot. Men with repeated legal hassles and run-ins with the cops, or who may have dangerous occupations, dazzle many women. Above all such a woman-pleaser should at least occasionally humiliate her and slap her around. Women will deny this ideal because they want men who are genuinely rich or brutal, not those who pretend to be. You won't be able to verify it from women's media, either, unless you can read between the lines, because all their public and semi-public communication is in Femspeak. To understand what lurks behind the verbal facade, think of all the guys you've known and ask which ones got the most.

You may be rich or well off, but if you're reading this, you're probably neither powerful nor a foreigner. If you're drug-addicted or violent you don't have much trouble forming and keeping relationships even with several women at the same time. If you're an honest, hard-working, productive citizen, however, most women regard you as a contemptible easy mark.

It's up to men, up to *you* to return cooperation and mutual respect to relationships since most women, whatever ethical precepts they may retain, find present circumstances too rewarding to change. They will improve only in response to actions beyond the scope of legislation and court rulings, and though we can't help them via the antisocial qualities fostered by matriarchy, there is one element of them we have to use.

Like scientists who deliberately treat the body as a machine for the compassionate purpose of fighting disease, men must drop their romantic, idealizing, often subservient attitude toward women and the negative opposite attitude it too often becomes. Instead we have to apply to women the same coldly objective, evaluative view that they have of all but the richest and most brutal men. Just as they ignore everything --- empathy, humor, interests, love of family, patriotism, *etc.* --- about men but the lowest common denominators, *i. e.*, that men must have property and have to work and are indeed motivated by lust, we have for this vital purpose to see women as motivated only by greed and social aspiration, as capable of feeling only anger, envy, pride, and resentment.

5

This goes against everything we've been taught and every social sanction, demanding great concentration. Even the exercise of looking at women's secondary divorce rewards may not be enough, and some men may have to overdo it, training themselves to see women's every word and deed right down to the subconscious functioning of their internal organs as deliberate, calculated maneuvers designed to get money and evade responsibility. Doing so is good preparation for the most difficult step of all: seeing how manipulation works and how women use it.

No Secrets

Besides recipes, romance tales, and makeup tips, women's media (like their conversations) include advice on manipulating men. We can verify this by looking through a few popular women's magazines like *Cosmopolitan* or *Glamour*. If we look at examples from the past fifteen years [before 1993] we'll also see that with men getting wise to their economic motives and purely sexual strategies, women have turned to pop psychology. "Intimacy" has become the manipulative buzzword. Women talk about "getting men to open up," to "express their feelings," and to tell all the secrets they're sure we all have and are hiding.

Wanting "intimacy" sounds caring and family oriented, and demanding it procures women more sympathy than they already receive. Men and women use the same language differently --- a fact women evade if they can't deny it; and men either shrug it off as proof women are flakes, or ignore it because it sounds like something a wimp would say. Women know men ignore this, and understand what men say about it and what men *think* women say; all of which confusion helps disguise women's "intimacy" psychobabble.

There aren't many objective studies of women's behavior, probably due to men's habitual idealization of them as well as because the scientific findings might contradict the feminist line that academics and social theorists have to follow, and because being objective about women appears "sexist" to the muddled majority. I'm going to interpret their language and actions on the assumption that women are rational, that they intend the results that benefit them, and fail only when chance or some personal flaw undoes their efforts.

If a woman says she likes honest men, for example, she *might* be telling the simple truth, and whatever she means, men think she wants them to spill their guts, explain their motives, tell all their plans, and be "sensitive." Actually, they are right, but there's usually more to it. She's also letting other women know she expects a man to be as popular and rich as he seems to be or that she wants one who is so emotionally stunted or so stupid that he's no problem to control.

"Intimacy" is part of women's way of testing people while entertaining themselves by enlarging ordinary, even trivial matters out of proportion; by pretending everyday happenings are the horrible faults of others. Combined with male idealization of women, all this makes it difficult for us to see the dangers of "intimacy." Men who don't see the contradiction of being tricked into being honest, or who don't understand the sensible reasons for controlling information about themselves are jeopardizing their marriages or other arrangements as well as their children, property, income, and way of life.

The very worst case, which looks pretty common since most marriages end in divorce and most divorces are filed by women, is where a man takes a woman's expectations at face value while the woman uses "intimacy" to sabotage the relationship. This can happen when a man tells his wife what she needs to know to play games with his feelings: she can make him look bad, keep him depressed or angry, provoke him to hit her, even drive him to drink or drugs. He may confess some deep secret such as the ones women are sure we all harbor, then she may react with disgust, outrage, revulsion, *etc.*, and get rid of him (but not his property). Or she may consider him weak for giving in to her demands for "intimacy."

Given a stable social setting, even when wives or girlfriends genuinely want permanence, "intimacy" usually ruins a healthy relationship. This is due to two basic features of female character that women try to hide from us. For one thing, they instinctively want men to be strong and protective. Under genteel civilized conditions, this most often means a man must be a hard worker if he's not rich. At the very least, men are generally expected to display the standard male virtues of someone who can take it, who doesn't give in, who doesn't show any weaknesses, and who overcomes failure.

If a man buckles to her demands for "intimacy," even if a woman honestly thinks she's doing what's best for both of them, she will feel deep inside that he is weak. She will be bothered by doubts about his manliness and about herself (is a wimp like this the best she can do?) She might never face, or even know what went wrong, but she'll automatically blame the man and make everyone involved miserable.

Feature number two, another side of their need for strong men, is women's desire to be mystified --- that is, symbolically overpowered. This is called their need for romance. Though they will usually idealize women, it's naturally easy for men to learn to see and like a particular woman as she is since a man automatically focuses on the physical person herself. In contrast, women are usually first attracted to superficialities of money and status, and by the fantasies concocted to fill in what is not known. While men's interest follows a logical course from physical to spiritual, much of what women do in a relationship consists of efforts to check their aspirations and imaginings against reality. It can take a lifetime revising illusions and rationalizing before a woman learns to appreciate the real person she married.

A man loses a lot of mystery when he lives with a woman, and there's no sense deliberately losing more. He can't hide biology. Habits stand out. Even if he's been a detective, a diplomat, a spy, a mercenary, or any combination thereof, he's had a finite number of experiences. If he says much about them, he'll end up repeating himself. Adding the "intimate" stuff one or both partners think she ought to know only uses up all the rest of the room the female's fantasy life needs. She'll soon be bored and quit investing time and energy trying to imagine or ferret out the man's "secrets." She won't be able to stay interested long enough to learn to care about the real person.

Trying to see if he'll weaken is part of this testing process, but not a part we should help women with. Instead, we have to watch out for the techniques she uses to do it. A woman ensures that her husband hears her tell another female that she's "trying to get him to open up." At the same time she's telling the other woman she's looking for his weaknesses, she's trying to get him to feel guilty for acting like a man. Another claims her mate is cold and insensitive, that she feels alone and worthless, that everyone needs companionship. In this case the wife is actually describing how the man would feel without her, playing upon his anxieties as well. This could mean that she has met someone else who interests her.

This example of reverse psychology brings us back to our worst case and the best reason not to get too "intimate": today's feminist dominated society. It's true everyone needs affection and companionship, but most women might as well not. They most often stay connected with family and female friends and they easily make friends. They're usually the center of male attention, never have to take the initiative (though it's okay if they do), and don't have to work for or pay for sex. All levels of government --- not to mention clubs, churches, charities, and businesses --- have rules favoring women and organizations designed to help only them.

Women's role has changed during the past two centuries and ours hasn't. Women, but not men, have been freed from traditional duties and limits without losing any traditional advantages. Men still expect their families to be havens of acceptance and affection while women, lacking any compulsory rules, now make marriage into power struggles ("sexual politics" in feminist argot). That's because women can support themselves while men are still forced to support them, giving wives extra leverage and ex-wives extra income. In fact, extra income is obviously the purpose of serial divorce practiced by some, if not most women.

Obviously, we know most women aren't evil. But they are human, and therefore prone to take advantage of situations and persons to the extent that they can operate outside the standard rules of conduct. And as Dr. Stanley Milgram showed in the 70s, completely normal persons will inflict pain on others as long as someone in authority tells them to or assures them it's all right. This is just human nature. We don't need to go into all the reasons gender roles have fallen into this state because they're beside the main point here. The important thing to know is that feminists have furnished the rhetoric to convince many women they don't have to obey the rules and legal authorities stand ready to reward women for acting according to feminist rhetoric.

Social subversives have put traditional male roles down because they are useful to us. B. F. Skinner, late dean of Behaviorist psychologists, explained how. Your opponent tries to weaken and discourage you. Any sign of either is a reward that encourages him or her to press the advantage. The lack of either is a discouragement. That's why self-control is everywhere a virtue: traditional male roles were designed to help us defend ourselves (and our countries) against enemies and disruptive social forces.

At present [1993], traditional roles are almost our only defense in a struggle we neither started nor deserve. "Intimacy" will furnish women with the knowledge they need to maneuver men around in relationships without their having to give anything in return. This will invite women to increase their manipulative behaviors rather than to cooperate with men, and the mere fact that this is so increases women's contempt and dislike for their victims. Normal male behavior is the only thing accessible to most men that can put a stop to this vicious cycle, and in the larger perspective of things it is all that can help reverse an otherwise inevitable decline of society.

"No Secrets" appeared in *Aladdin's Window* # 11, edited by J. R. Molloy. Copyright 1993 by David C. Morrow.

Female Indecisiveness

Women's seeming indecisiveness is a conscious maneuver that helps them evade responsibility and, whenever possible, shifts that responsibility to men. Indecisiveness accords with the traditional falsehood that women are incompetent and weak, even stupid, and need male guidance. Women actually have no trouble making up their minds because they know what they like and what they want; a woman has usually reached her decision well before she tries to make it look like a man made it for her.

On some level most men suspect women's behavior in decision situations, but seldom see its purpose or how it works. If you've ever tried to get a female to state even a trivial preference you've probably been frustrated by her incessant qualifications and arguments against her own statements, repeated insistence it makes no difference, and suggestions (or accusations) that you're weak --- even if you tried it back when feminists were "demanding the right" to make their own decisions. The same woman most likely made her choices known later in an angry tirade that "defied" your having "forced" her to do whatever she'd finally agreed to, or maybe as a plea that if only you'd listened to her...

She may stage the fit without having made a choice because you were "too weak or indecisive" to tell her what to do. The reason for this behavior, which would cause a man to be diagnosed as hopelessly neurotic or anti-social, is that the female wants to avoid the personal responsibility she has constantly pretended to demand, so she gets upset if she suspects you've seen through her games. Since she isn't honest, it doesn't occur to her that you are.

Women's indecisive behavior supports their traditional image and sets men up for various games. Really naïve men react to their vacillation with natural egoism. In our society this is intensified by the doctrine of female superiority; men are flattered to help a superior being and are brainwashed to believe themselves worthless without female attention. Whether she is really concerned with or indifferent to the issue on which a woman "needs" a man's help, the result is predictable. She has in either case decided what she wants before she sets out to maneuver a man into seeming to decide for her --- a choice, as she intends, for which he will be held responsible. If she succeeds, she is gratified and looks on him with contempt because she can control him (as she wants to do), while if she fails she is enraged and admires him.

If her choice turns out to have been wrong, the man "forced" it on her, while if it turns out right she either let him think he made it to protect his "male ego" or had to fight his efforts to make her do something else. If she sees in time it is wrong, chivalry and the superstition that women are irrational yet mysteriously wise frees them to change it. A woman sometimes gets a man to make the wrong decision so she can show her power to other females as well as to him. If a man tries to "let" or "encourage" her to choose because of her tirades against "male dominance," she will use the situation to make him feel unmanly for not forcing her to accept his decision.

Pretended indecision serves further purposes. When a woman appears confused, excited, or vulnerable, or acts silly or stupid, it arouses sexual interest and so makes men more easily controlled and more easily frustrated. It can thus spark male rivalries. Women put men in decision situations to evaluate their intelligence and pliability and show off to other females. Men's confident taking charge of spurious dilemmas amuses women, all the more so when the man knows the problem is ridiculous, especially when he suspects the woman does too.

By making a man wait for her to pretend to make up her mind, a woman signals her superior social status; refinements include rejecting his help after she's asked for it, and finally acting on one of his suggestions while claiming, often in rebellious defiance, that it was really her idea. In the same vein, women often terminate indecision with sudden "uncharacteristic" actions that, while consistent with their repeated inconsistencies and mysteriousness, is usually seen as desperate. Witnesses are usually surprised and impressed.

Female indecisiveness, in short, isn't cute or sexy. At best it may show genuine concern for a legitimate cause, but that's a rare occasion with a rare woman. In the vast majority of cases it shows up a woman as dishonest, lazy, or manipulative in some combination, or as just plain stupid. Any woman who puts on a show of being unable to make up her mind, or who actually can't, is best avoided. You can live without her, but, especially considering the costs of divorce, you'd have a hard time living with her.

False Problems: A Women's Divorce Tool

Divorce is most American women's goal. To arrange divorces, which they plan as carefully as they do weddings, women use several strategies. Beyond feminist fads involving fairly rare and potentially disprovable acts like child sexual abuse and wife beating, their most common tool in this age of psychobabble [1998] is false problems.

We all know its basis, women's routine claims of multitudes of difficulties. Examples include fake stupidity and pretending to be unable to decide what clothes or makeup to wear. Women in general are not stupid and when alone have no trouble making decisions, an act they put on only in relationship contexts. In our latter instance a woman's purpose might be to exasperate her husband into a bad humor so he will attend a social event in unwitting support of her allegations he's a jerk.

False problems are especially useful with that most difficult of men, the nice, kind, hardworking fellow who takes care of her and the kids. Men's general decency and integrity present women with profound difficulties, and to aid in overcoming these feminists claim that women are "more emotionally aware and insightful." This integrates into poppsych drivel the belief that although weak and stupid women are "mysterious" and "wise."

The wife acts troubled and confused and declares "her" marriage to have terrible problems of which her husband is either unaware due to "male insensitivity," is in denial, or callously indifferent. Her word will be accepted and the husband's supposed blindness or obstinacy taken as examples of what's causing the difficulty. His surprise, which proves his insensitivity if not his downright malignity, is caused by his ignorance of the only real problem: his wife's scheme to divorce. That, combined with women's high status and *carte blanche* to lie automatically put him on the defensive.

Men are usually uncertain about "psychological" matters and avoid criticizing women, especially their wives. Hesitation elicits a wife's contempt since she knows she is lying and like all women despises weak or chivalrous men. Others see it as a symptom or an indirect admission of guilt or both. If a man realizes he is caught in a web of lies and deceit and that our gender system is a farce, he may become angry --- which "proves" he is causing the problems. A husband's failure to even see the nonexistent problems or his naturally futile attempts to deal with them, or his anger all "prove" they are totally his fault. Out of chivalry, stupidity, or hopes of money or sex other men will claim to believe the wife.

Problems real or concocted enable women to use one of their most potent anti-family tools: counseling. Women use counseling because it brings in feminist reinforcements whose job is to find problems, also because they hope to find out things about the husband they never knew without revealing anything real about themselves. Counseling is a more or less public degradation of the man that shakes his confidence, stigmatizes, and isolates him.

A wife who seeks counseling *appears* to be trying to save a marriage, which is an automatic indictment of a husband who never considered it (since there aren't any problems except the wife). Husbands who don't want counseling are doing nothing or even resisting any effort to "save" "her" marriage. If a husband goes, he loses more of the wife's respect because he can't stand on his own two feet and cause her to hate him for being strong. If he does not give in she admires his persistence in his evil scheme to preserve his self-respect and his family, which stubborn "uncooperativeness" and "lack of insight" proves him at fault.

Counseling documents only the husband as a personal failure, since by poppsych doctrine only men cause trouble and women cannot be blamed or even criticized for anything. Even if a wife undeniably does have mental difficulties they aren't her responsibility but one of her husbands' or maybe her father's (or one of her mother's husbands'), so she is still utterly innocent. Since the counseling will add to the accusations already leveled and since he will be blamed even if the woman does openly reveal her own shortcomings and they outweigh his ("he drove me nuts"), the relationship will be hastened toward dissolution by what in our society is not therapy, but a ritual that absolves women and blames men.

In or out of counseling women don't tell anyone except female confidants their real motives unless doing so would make a man look bad or ridiculous. That's because their motives are to get property settlements and support payments from as many men as possible. They needn't tell female counselors, who like female friends and relatives are sources of advice and support, since these reasons are understood.

While women may give false reasons to make men look bad and themselves look good and to maneuver husbands into actions seeming to justify the breakup they often give none even when doing so wouldn't hurt their cause. Male silence is usually tact or chivalry, but women's is quite different. As a manipulative ploy silence allows a victim to "fill in the blanks," letting him imagine things that may induce him to act submissive as well as further discredit himself. Another reason is to leave open the possibility of reconciliation if the woman's new affair falls through or the ex gets rich or famous. Most women consider themselves too important to explain themselves to men, especially men so lowly as to be rejected. Finally, women remain silent to reinforce the myth that they are mysterious and inexplicable, rendering questions about them beyond and none of mere mortals' business.

"False Problems: A Women's Divorce Tool" has not appeared elsewhere.

Role Ambiguity As Manipulation

Most women seem as unhappy with their now [1986] ambiguous social situation as some have been with traditional limitations. One cause of this ambiguity is the continuation of outdated behavior by both women and certain authorities who have learned to use the confusions of change as tools for personal profit and the furtherance of feminist extremism. Contemporary America provides special opportunities and incentives for them to do so at men's expense.

Though women were once restricted from full legal adulthood, they enjoyed such compensations as chivalry, special legal considerations, exemption from public duties, and emotional freedom. As legislative and judicial action democratically broadened their rights, and technology created jobs no longer requiring gross strength, women retained their old compensations. Men, however, have been compelled to maintain their roles as provider and soldier, and stay within the restrictions of antiquated values while enjoying no new rights or compensations.

Since women can now support themselves and no longer suffer from the stigma of being a single mother, they don't have to be married. However, the law still forces men to divide their property with, and continue to support, ex-wives and children they may seldom see, and usually to finance the initial divorce.

David Allen, R. F. Doyle, and Monte Vanton, among others, have shown the perverse chivalry and sometimes outright corruption behind favoritism toward women in civil law. In March 1981 attorney Marvin Mitchelson, of palimony notoriety, won the case of *Maynard vs. Priester* for a non-live-in mistress seeking support from her married lover. And in *Fleming vs. Fleming*, the Kansas Supreme Court ruled that although the ex-wife was living out of wedlock with her boyfriend to avoid losing alimony by remarriage, and although unmarried cohabitation was illegal in Kansas, Mr. Fleming had to continue financing the arrangement.

Criminal law is the same. A recent U. S. General Accounting Office survey shows that for the same offense men are twice as likely to be sentenced to prison, that women's sentences are always shorter, and that women are less likely to receive prison sentences for murder. Dr. Coramae Mann, Florida criminologist, notes that the more serious the offense the lighter will be a woman's sentence compared to a man's. In *The Rape of the Male* R. F. Doyle cites a public prosecutor's admission that when a couple is arrested, policy is to "get the man" and free the woman.

Most men are good citizens, conditioned to loyalty, who find it hard to admit that the law is prejudiced, much less sometimes an outright scam. Lifelong teaching that women are angelic, with unfathomable minds and eternally noble motives, implies that men are the opposite. Realistic men know, whether they admit it or not, that the relationships with women the deck is stacked against them. They keep quiet to minimize their losses.

Men strive for success, are crushed by failure, and are isolated --- whether they win or lose --- by others' envy or contempt. Women, however, may compete if they wish, cop out at any time, are overpraised if they succeed, and accepted if they fail. Women enjoy great latitude in dress, manners, and lifestyle, while men must stick to strict codes. Intellectuals like Ashley Montague preach female superiority while the media idealize women and portray men as brutes or buffoons. A result is the double standard that creates opportunities for sexual manipulation. Women, who can enter half naked into places from which men are excluded for lacking ties, enjoy special protective laws against rape, exposure to men's bodies, and discrimination.

Fitting fist in glove with female privilege and male debasement is the feminist teaching that men are mere animals driven solely by lust for sex and power. This rationalization enables them to use either traditional or liberated behavior as it suits them. For example, if a woman wins a legal case it is by reason of her superiority; but if she loses the case, it is because of the machinations of the sexist "patriarchal" system. A promiscuous woman is exercising the right to control her own body until trouble arises, in which case she's seeking love and men are using her or else she can't help herself because of what men have done to her. Women don't commit crimes, but if they do and get caught, they're victims of the "patriarchal" system, or their husbands/boyfriends made them do it, or they simply don't understand the complex legislation created by the brilliant minds of those big strong men.

Exactly what do manipulative women do to maneuver us into divorce court and other such positions which are lucrative for them and damaging to us? They use masculine vulnerabilities: the nature of our sex drive, lifelong training in chivalry, an ethic demanding the suppression of feeling and the pursuit of only certain achievements, and our resulting inner conflicts. Against these inner conflicts women bring their wide range of permissible feelings and behavior, and lifelong practice at understanding intimate relationships.

In America, the constant male sex drive is kept on an adolescent and promiscuous level by the belief the men are animals who can barely restrain themselves and must give in to their sex drives, whatever the cost, at any opportunity. It is further supported by our fear of homosexuality and drive to achieve. We thus end up as sexual rivals, which then forces us to seek emotional closeness only with women.

More difficult to deal with is chivalry. During infancy, when women are the most important other, men are forced to regard them as special and superior beings, mysterious and inexplicable, whose power mustn't be underestimated though they are weak, delicate, illogical, and need protection. Since it is an integral part of the ethic requiring men to deny themselves and work for others, chivalry creates anger toward women by forcing men to treat them as objects, thus denying that women can be understood as persons and thereby excusing them from responsibility. This begins in childhood when, although girls are boys' physical equals, we are told we mustn't fight them however much they hit, scratch, bite, lie, cheat, or steal. Boys soon enough learn girls' invulnerability lies in adult protection, which boys must provide as they become men. This trade off only increases anger. Women, then, signal men to be chivalrous by acting silly, weak, or irrational, or bursting into tears, or blaming other men. Naturally, many a male's chivalrous facade hides contempt and hatred, and as a result the chivalrous man seldom cares to understand women beyond what is necessary to screw them.

An example in which the code of chivalry is used to manipulate men, one that clearly shows the use of role ambiguity, was recently committed by Suzanne Somers. A few years ago she entered into a modeling contract with Playboy Enterprises, agreeing to pose for them in exchange for a stated sum and, apparently, a trip to the Mexican photographic location. As a liberated woman controlling her own body, Somers was exercising her rights as an adult, and when she became famous the pictures' owners decided to use their legitimate rights to publish them in *Playboy* magazine. Suddenly Somers was a hurt, terribly wronged lady publicly declaring her humiliation at how those awful men had used her. Though she was now rich, though she had no legal claim to further payment, Hefner (who made his fortune exploiting male sexuality through the idealization of women) played Knight in Shining Armor and lavishly rewarded her tantrum.

Hardest to change are the purely psychological factors which make men vulnerable to manipulation. Besides having to idealize women while using them, men must repress their own emotions and feelings and seek intimacy only with women. Unaware of much of their own selves, and having to regard interest in male persons as trivial or self-indulgent, if not a symptom of homosexuality, many men may end up ignorant about their emotions. Lack of emotional training then works against them when they do try to understand women, burdened as they are by the notion that females do no wrong. If a woman cries, for example man is likely to blame himself and believe she is suffering the same intensity of pain necessary to make him cry; his overreaction will doubtless be to her profit.

Women's basic manipulative strategies are to keep the man in doubt or double bind situations and to get him to act out repressed anger in such a way as to make him look bad before others. For example, the manipulative woman may work hard to please her husband with menial tasks, keeping him interested in her while appearing to do her part. Then, right before company comes she will pick an argument. Since her anger is false she can easily drop it to act frightened or stoic, but since his is real he stays mad, giving proof to the woman's friends of his nastiness and her decency.

There are many other such tactics. She may constantly combine his likes and dislikes, for example bringing up unpleasant topics or procrastinating at dinner or bed time. She may privately share his interests while telling friends he imposes them on her. She may pretend to like something she will later despise when he gets it for her, or be vague or equivocal about her preferences so he will always be wrong ("Oh, you just don't understand!"). She may interfere with his habits or schedule, "expect" him to do things he can't, or act surprised when he accomplishes something. She may accept his intimate confessions only to reveal them, or threaten to, or act disgusted by them precisely when he feels most vulnerable.

Since this female behavior is supposedly either an oppressed person's efforts at emancipation or the traditional prerogative of "weak, irrational" females, the women can't lose. Since the man generally lacks support, and wouldn't accept it anyway, he most often loses, however right or decent he may be. If he's tolerant, he encourages her. If he resists, he's a brute. Even others who are aware of the game will probably blame him, and since he's so confused emotionally he'll probably blame himself, too. His only recourse, it often appears, is to become colder, more repressed, and callous, which paradoxically (and self-destructively) makes him even more attractive to women.

"Why is it," wrote *Redbook* Editorial Assistant Cathy Cavender in a 19 June 1979 letter to me, "that women prefer cold, domineering men to the thoughtful, sensitive ones? It isn't an easy question to answer. Perhaps it has to do with the fact that, just as society has encouraged men to be unemotional or 'masculine,' it has upheld this same kind of man as an object of love

"And, just as men must make an effort to free themselves from this limiting stereotype, women must overcome the model society has set for them and become open to emotional sensitive men."

Ms. Cavender is eminently right, but why don't more women assume their own responsibilities? Because, unlike men, they don't have to if they don't want to. A woman's passivity forces her partner to do the work, run the risks, make the mistakes, and bear the consequences.

When a man treats a woman in a sensitive, considerate manner her probable reaction once she realizes he isn't gay is loathing and contempt. Since male sensitivity is considered a weakness, many women fear having to carry some of the responsibility in a relationship with a sensitive man. Unfortunately, some sensitive men actually are weak, partly because the trauma of masculine upbringing emotionally cripples them. And a few women prefer weak men, whom they nevertheless despise, because they are easily dominated yet still must bear legal responsibilities.

So a sensitive man who is strong and confident is just as likely to be hated as the brutish ultra-macho man. Obviously most feminists don't like sensitive men, but neither do plenty of other women. Not only might such a man expect women to behave responsibly, but if he sees women as human rather than celestial beings he isn't necessarily vulnerable to manipulation. The last thing a manipulative woman wants is to be understood; she doesn't want someone who can see through her games.

Since sincere feminists have worked hard for two decades to get women accepted as responsible autonomous persons, and since the majority of women have wasted their efforts by remaining manipulative rather than becoming responsible grown-ups, it is now up to men to help women by helping ourselves.

A first step is to stop taking the blame for women's problems and stop tolerating the vilification of heterosexual men. It is never necessary and it is always harmful to accept women's debasing judgments of ourselves. Responsibility for men's and women's problems lies with those who manipulate the law and the media, and the way to deal with them is to direct our anger outwardly through activism. American law and opinion are accessible. The same means used by other interest groups, including feminists, can be used by men: letter campaigns directed toward legislators, publicizing judicial abuses, protesting or boycotting the sponsors of television shows that belittle males and glorify parasitic women. Persistence, exposure, and the imaginative use of every possible pretext, and education are the keys to public success.

On a one-to-one basis, female manipulative strategies depend largely upon a woman's ability to arouse concern for her pretended weakness and inferiority --- these strategies evoke chivalry and infatuation. A logical approach to this might be to claim that since feminists say women are superior it is therefore we biologically, legally, and socially disadvantaged men who can claim special consideration.

But a more useful approach is to see through women's games. Rational scientific work can help us in this task. Freud's associate Alfred Adler early recognized that a majority of those who appear to be suffering from neurotic disorders actually benefit from them in ways that escape notice by their supposedly fortunate kin. Seeming incompetent and weak, Adler showed, can actually bring someone attention and power by arousing others' guilt and compassion. On different levels psychiatrists like Thomas Szasz and Eric Berne have continued to explore these games. From this and our own observations we can conclude that the social conditioning which some persons learned in childhood and still suffer from may yet be performed for personal profit.

Consistently treating women as responsible adults will help them become such, but to do so we must solve our own ambiguity problems. We are conditioned to take pride in believing ourselves to be nearly helpless slaves of our sex drives. But obviously men can control their sexuality; otherwise society could not function. Peacetime armies could not be maintained or disbanded because the soldiers, doubtless joined by peace officers, would use their weapons to maintain continuous orgies. Rape would most often be committed, or attempted, by boys twelve to eighteen because during adolescence, when self-discipline and foresight are still immature, the male sex drive is strongest.

The male animal delusion favors feminist sexism, flatters the super-macho, and gives wimps, i.e. male apologists, a rationale. Reared to assume responsibilities and repress themselves, the latter may accept feminist vituperation and turn their own anger inward.

But we must realize that passive, feminist masculinity does not liberate us because, like the super-macho ideal, it is based on the same belief that men are evil. The opposite of the vulnerable male is the strong sensitive type so many women dislike. Aware of his own feelings and genuine interests, such a man is free of sexual doubt and hence wastes none of his time proving himself sexually. He chooses female companions on the basis of their personal qualities, treats them as they merit, and isn't afraid to turn down sex. Able to take on responsibilities, he doesn't automatically assume blame, but he deals with problems where they actually lie. In respecting himself, he isn't open to manipulation, while by treating others as responsible persons he helps free them from their stereotyped roles and confusions.

"Role Ambiguity as Manipulation" appeared in *Transitions* Volume 7, Number 5, September/October 1986. Copyright 1986 by David C. Morrow.

How Women Manipulate

Ideally, relationships are equal. Equality is fragile and fairly rare; a few persons like and respect each other enough to create it, but it's usually the result of defined roles and tradeoffs, i. e. "I'll bear and rear your children if you'll support and protect us." Most often people try to dominate others and every organization is to some extent hierarchical. The military, and to a lesser degree businesses are examples of designed hierarchies. To get a larger perspective, feudalism isn't the opposite of democracy since it balances statuses with mutual obligations. Absolute monarchies and totalitarian states are their respective opposites. In hierarchies and whenever standards break down people's normal self-interest causes a struggle for dominance, which is what's happening I our gender situation and why we're mainly concerned with informal interpersonal struggles.

People who try to control others are here called *aggressors* and those they attack *victims*. Aggressors use four methods we can term, in order of increasing subtlety, *coercion*, *extortion*, *manipulation*, and *habituation*. Our main interest is how women use manipulation and habituation, but the first two methods are also important and are easier to understand.

With few exceptions only governments can use coercion, which here means injuring and killing victims, and they use it to take advantage of weaker states as well as for internal regulation. Criminals use it for profit, sex, fun, and such attendant purposes as eliminating witnesses. Coercion usually brings quick results. Most victims try to minimize their pain and few witnesses will risk victimization. Unless totally helpless, victims must be quickly overcome so they won't escape or harm the aggressor, and may be so badly damaged they become useless except as entertainment or examples. Victims will fight back if enough are attacked or even threatened often enough, especially by coercion not used according to accepted rules or if the aggressor has underestimated them.

Despite the usual corruption the United States' built in limits to government coercion work fairly well except in certain areas. The IRS is a familiar example. Another is psychiatrists, who can not only impose stigmatizing labels but imprison, drug, shock, and operate on persons whether or not they actually need it. A tendency not controlled in many societies, though the Communists' struggles against "cults of personality" seems to have been an attempt, is for aggressors to become heroes. Chivalry is our prime example. Women are generally not punished for violence and feminists have worked to extend the privilege. Now women can not only cut out and kill men's unborn children but maim and murder men on the basis of "date rape" and "recovered memories."

Extortion is the use of threat. It may be set up by coercion but is often indirect, as when the aggressor convinces victims that obedience is the way to avoid disease, fear, loneliness, or the like. The IRS is again an example; though it can prosecute, it usually relies on the desire to avoid threats and repetitions of bureaucratic procedures. Employers use fear of losing home, family, and future not only to get people to work and follow rules but to harass them for fun. Extortion can be a custom. Men can be forced into the military by threats of prison and death while women can't.

Since it's not as immediately destructive as coercion, extortion can be long lasting. It can accelerate into violence if the victim despairs or gains an advantage; the famous Charles Atlas ads are a pop culture depiction of this. A victim's resources may be consumed, as when a protection racket bankrupts a "client" or insurance rates rise too high to be affordable. An aggressor may become dependent on the victim like the pampered elite unable to survive without servants.

Manipulation and habituation form a different category of control methods because they aren't directly based on the survival instinct. Manipulation, instead, uses the social and individual motives that psychologist Abraham Maslow called "higher needs" and claimed came to the fore when a person was safe and healthy. This is what gives manipulation its peculiar advantage.

Manipulation has a single basis to which six strategies are applied, usually in various combinations. Fundamental, most important and oddly difficult to grasp, is that it uses what people *want*, not what they *need*. People will simply take what they need and if they are threatened their survival instinct will eventually take over even if futile or suicidal, but most will play by the rules to get what they want and only *try harder if told they can't have it*. This is why luxuries, which are useless or at least superfluous, are expensive and necessities cheap, and why few people will steal or kill to marry or social climb or get rich, which makes crime news and manipulation relatively safe.

Since it uses victims' personal motives and traits, manipulation often appears to them as well as to others to be their voluntary self-serving activity rather than an aggressor's attack. Manipulation doesn't necessarily consume victims' strength and resources, thus allowing them to be ridden and cheated for decades of otherwise productive lives. There's no inbuilt defense since being manipulated, like having a neurosis, is actually a form of self-actualization that doesn't work as intended. Overcoming manipulation, often even becoming aware of it, therefore requires hard and likely embarrassing work and defense against it tends to look like pettiness or ingratitude if not an unwarranted attack on an innocent person or helpful friend.

Likely the most difficult to see of the six strategies is use of victims' consistencies and repetitions. Most activities, however complex, from driving to work to distinctive mannerisms are habitual and unconscious. Manipulators interfere with habits to cause anger or anxiety and accommodate them to arouse feelings of security and companionship. Since people are reluctant to discuss habits even if aware of them, and look silly accusing someone of interfering with or imitating them, they can for example be easily hurt while made to appear ill tempered via habit blocking. Institutions establish routines not only for efficiency, but to create and so control such unconscious behavior.

Another strategy is isolation. Isolation prevents victims' drawing moral or even physical help from others. It hides manipulative techniques and aggressors' real motives. Isolation increases a victim's self-consciousness, anxiety, feelings of helplessness, often to painful degrees. In this state he may reveal fears and hopes to an aggressor who will as the scam requires make him feel worse or offer consolation to strengthen their supposed bonds. To destroy credibility the aggressor may abuse and insult the isolated victim so the latter will express negative, angry feelings toward her or simply describe her behavior objectively to persons around whom the aggressor has always acted perfectly respectable, if not charming.

Isolation doesn't necessarily mean that the action is physically hidden or even subtle, but often that witnesses are habitually or willfully blind to it or see the victim as lacking credibility. As seen in the discussion of coercion, the best way to isolate someone is frequently to attack him openly. Nobody wants to be next or get involved in personal disputes, and by nature most want to join a straightforward aggressor. Only persons' blood relatives have any automatic tendency to defend them, and most Americans live in nuclear, now monoparent or pastiche families having few actual kin, while the professionals who are supposed to help us operate by bureaucratic regulations and social fads.

Criminals obviously must use it, but isolation is a social as well as an individual technique. It is one function of class, racism, and other institutions regulating who can be defended and hurt. Employees' economic needs isolate them. Almost nobody would rescue a white American's black victim between Reconstruction and the Civil Rights Movement. As we'll see, men are also institutionally isolated.

A third strategy, frequently in use when women act capricious or fickle or when they pretend to be stupid or mysterious, is ambiguity. The victim is kept uncertain as to whether he will get what he wants. Ambiguity has a dual purpose rooted in certain clearly understood mental operations. It strengthens motivation just as does a challenge and maintains it just as the possibility of winning keeps a gambler running against the probability of losing. This aspect is an example of what learning theorists call *intermittent reinforcement*; actions that are only frequently rewarded seldom cease, while those that are always reinforced stop almost as soon as the reward. Ambiguity can also get victims to reveal themselves when they appear to act on purely conscious, objective intent. Here it corresponds to psychologists' use of *projective tests*. A person asked to describe in detail some vague stimulus --- an unfinished drawing, a sentence fragment --- will usually rely on personal mental constructs to fill the gaps.

Information control, from simple omissions to misleading words to outright lies to elaborate charades, is another strategy and one needing little explanation. The manipulator must of course seldom reveal her true motives and even less so her methods. Although the victim may actually accept and ignore or rationalize her motives, the personal truth of being manipulated can be so demeaning it might turn him to violence. Obviously disinformation also gets the victim to do, even think, what the aggressor wants.

Akin to disinformation is the use of suggestion. The strategy works especially well with ambiguity and when the aggressor enjoys some level of power outside the manipulative situation. It consists of repetitions of words or phrases, interpreting or implying interpretations of behavior and situations, or repeatedly displaying selected emotions, the creation of some specific ambiance by means of location or music or clothes or drink or the like.

Suggestion operates on emotion and intellect alike. We aren't conscious of everything of which we are aware and probably can't be, so the brain is hard wired to automatically process input and bring to attention only what seems either threatening or relevant to what we're doing. Imitation and example are fundamental to learning and shared behavior is to social life, activities we can handle unconsciously, so as a matter of course we take cues without thinking or even knowing about it from authorities and those emotionally important to us. Most even of what we can deliberately control is, as students of Gurdjieff insist, automatic and managed from outside our minds. We'll give examples of these two methods below.

The sixth strategy, actually already described along with the others, is reward and punishment. Since it is well understood in both everyday life and psychological theory, it needs little explanation. In particular, the manipulator doles out what the victim wants; behaviorists aptly term this "shaping behavior" through *operant conditioning*, which means rewarding actions the victim chooses to perform that resemble, and thereby increasingly resemble, what the aggressor wants him to do. In manipulation, however, unlike in discipline or teaching, the victim must usually be unaware of his conditioning or at least that it is deliberately contrived.

Habituation here refers to the controllability someone brings to a situation. It can be the outcome of convention or of individual experience, and some persons may be naturally more submissive than others. Conventional, or customary habituation is fostered through child rearing practices and such institutions as church and school, and reinforced by adage, entertainment, even legal compulsion. Chivalry is the most important to our concerns, but military training is easy to grasp. Habituation to a specialized authority structure for the purpose of military efficiency begins upon induction and is carried through subsequent military experience.

As the result of personal experiences, habituation usually stunts personal growth whether it develops unconsciously or deliberately. Aggressors look for habitual victims since these aren't likely to fight back or seek help and may not realize they're being used. Such persons may live as the uncomprehending victim of a series of bullies, scam artists, and violent criminals.

A child reared with relentless criticism may never make decisions and a man reared by a domineering mother may be automatically submissive to women. Such men may never realize their plight or they may believe that women are superior. Some, like the guy who hires a dominatrix, may separate that part of themselves from the rest of their lives. Habituation may result from a decision to follow the path of least resistance in a situation. Mechanical obedience to a wife's nagging may be easier than listening to it, cheaper than divorce, and temporarily shut her up.

Habituation can break down. Social habituation involving millions of people over centuries yields to changes in such basics as religion and technology. Slavery was increasingly seen to violate Christian and democratic ideals, and it couldn't outproduce mechanized industry, either. When it fell, arrays of accustomed, seemingly everlasting routine behavior ceased, in some areas in far less than a lifetime. Personal habituation may pass as a matter of course when children come to support themselves. Intentionally or not, individuals break it by relocating, joining organizations, changing interests. Success (financial especially) can alter it.

When victims improve, aggressors may run through the entire control gamut trying to stop them. A wife, for example, will go from manipulation through marriage counseling even to physical assault to keep a husband from becoming a whole person. Violence is possible; an employee struggling to improve against a boss who harasses him may snap, leaving people to wonder why so nice and hardworking a person would kill everyone at the office.

How do women use these methods against men? To understand, it's vital to see the basics objectively and in their larger context. The manipulator --- or, in our cases, the manipulatrix --- must have or appear to have something the victim wants: fame, information, money, secret knowledge, sex...Not *needs*, but *wants*. The manipulatrix tries to get her victim, you, to feel that only she can provide it, to believe you need her, and to forget you can choose.

In reality you *want* a particular woman but you don't *need* her. If men needed certain women, courtship would entail simply finding them. There would be no adultery, no harems, no hookers, no remarried widows and widowers. Blasphemous as it sounds, you don't even *need* sex, you *want* it. If sex were a need, anyone deprived of it would die within a predictable span after going through a predictable sequence of symptoms and could up to a predictable point be revived by it just as happens to people without food or water. Sex is not vital because choice, whether between peacocks' tails or women's breast sizes, is important in mating. This *sexual selection* is the essence of at least vertebrate reproduction and is what makes sex amenable to cultural and personal modification. What you have to bear in mind is that if you don't get any you won't even get sick, much less die, so you don't have to perform for it.

Women try to control men in general by such means as clothes and body language, and the effort intensifies in relationships. They don't have to seek men who are personally habituated to submit to females because in addition to wanting them for sex, children, and family life as nature urges, Western or at least American men have culturally fostered attitudes that create the same effect. Women's goal is not marriage but serial divorce, because that's how they get free property and unearned income.

Feminists' spate of pretending to demand the "right" to make the first move was just that: a pretense for manipulative purposes. Most women have no intention of openly initiating an encounter, but follow the tradition of getting men to. They usually use abbreviated sexual preening movements to do this rather than talking, which would show an interest in a man as a person, including making and dropping eye contact, licking their lips, touching their hair, adjusting their posture, and rubbing themselves. A woman thus ambiguously signals to a man that she *might* give him something if he makes the right effort, though this ambiguity is situational in that the more wealth and status the man has vis a vis her the more blatant and silly the woman's behavior. Not only is this strictly and safely according to custom but it begins a potential relationship with a successful act of manipulation that leaves the female without definable responsibility. If he responds, a man becomes obligated for and encouraged by any rewards and the more time and effort he invests the more determined he's likely to become.

Still today a relationship's early phases are largely predictable, not only because of courtship custom but of the common situation these customs simplify. Things remain positive, though the female begins to plant the seeds of destruction, so until the couple has a more definite knowledge of each other and especially until the female gets the man to make some kind of commitment or perceives that he has, ambiguity and reward-punishment predominate.

A woman uses ambiguity to test a man and keep him uncertain while establishing herself as mysterious. As she gradually suits her behavior to the relationship and establishes control she acts variously capricious, cold, emotional, fickle, moody, rigid, dependent and self-reliant, dropping what doesn't work (perhaps to throw it up to him later as an example of how he "controlled her" or "made her repress herself"). A part of this men seldom grasp is women's use of reward and rejection not only to shape their behavior and get them to do things women will later claim to hate, but to confuse them by using it at random. However, sex and affection must in most cases proceed along a definite trajectory of increasing intimacy --- or apparent intimacy --- since otherwise most men would lose interest.

Disinformation and suggestion are at every stage women's most used strategies. Easily improvised and too trivial in most cases to complain about, they can support complicated campaigns. Women lie even when there's no possible need to, and confidently since they're never punished and from childhood practice on males they don't like. Men are taught by chivalry to believe them even when the lie is obvious, especially their emotional statements, and are afraid confrontation will alienate not only the female but everyone else.

Further, women collaborate on lies, working out routines, and will back up or "unknowingly" support others' tales, interpret their words and deeds "behind their backs" and "in strictest confidence" and supply "information" at crucial times. ("She didn't attack you in front of everyone. She's afraid you don't really like her/afraid of so-and-so/had PMS and was too embarrassed to say so/didn't know what to say/was so upset...") To keep in practice and remain consistent women arbitrarily lie about their motives and feelings --- the latter usually being faked to begin with. Lying about external reality is more difficult, but in addition to female support they also use truth mixed with falsehood.

Women use their high status and traditional roles to defend against the relationship watershed of lie detection. If questioned they add more lies mixed with truth, acting silly or confused, and if that doesn't work they'll claim to be insecure or even stupid. They may launch an appeal based on their "low self-esteem" or whatever the current line is, or claim to have been lying to spare someone's feelings. By female lore men find such tiresome and boring behavior as stupidity to be sexy and therefore distracting.

Also based on tradition are appeals to awe and pulling rank. Women may throw tantrums and emotional tirades, pretend to be so offended they burst into tears, even act innocent. They credit their lies to mysterious female reasons men can't grasp, and it's a dead giveaway she knows a man's onto her when a woman says, "Oh, you just don't understand!" As we'll see, my assertion that women consciously use such devices isn't just based on anecdotal evidence, but can be directly supported by feminist writings.

Lie detection rouses women to rage and hatred because it removes their power and so destroys a relationship before she's ready: if you forgive or tactfully overlook a lie a woman will consider you weak and stupid and get rid of you as profitably as she can, while if you confront her she'll admire and respect you as she destroys the relationship --- because she expects to be superior in every way --- by painting you as aggressor and herself as innocent victim.

Aggressors seldom limit themselves to verbal lies. Women imitate or complement a victim's body language and mannerisms to evoke feelings of companionship or security, and will use counter movements to cause discomfort, feelings whose source and certainly whose purpose he will seldom realize. Women may make a man feel threatened by talking loudly while waving or flexing their arms, a tactic of many male bullies, but rather than to intimidate men women may do it to get men to attack them. Women will go around looking distressed or frightened and deny, quite truthfully, that there's anything wrong. They may prefer to look depressed or disappointed and deny it, and in every such case others' assumption will of course be that her husband, boyfriend, or some likely male is the cause. Body language as well as coquettish talk is widely used to tease men into doing women favors and get them to make advances that can cause useable rivalry or be repulsed.

Women normally intend prenuptial disinformation to make themselves look good to their victims, while after the ceremony they use it to make their husbands look bad to everyone else. There are many everyday examples of the latter. Before company arrives a wife screams at her husband in pretended rage. When guests appear he's angry but she either acts sweet and thoughtful or worried, even frightened, all easily done since she wasn't really upset at all. In his presence she might mention to others in disgusted or enraged tones some embarrassing or incriminating secret her husband has confided, perhaps attributing it to a movie character or tabloid celebrity. This will hurt and threaten him privately, possibly upset him before witnesses. Lies are a favorite telephone device. A man discusses something innocent with his wife who, on the other end of the lie and with witnesses, pretends she's sobbing quietly or acts as though trying to deal with a vicious tirade. She may burst into tears and hang up. If there's nobody around to witness her behavior, she may scream abuse at him or say something cutting and hang up.

The typical divorce scheme also requires that women make men unhappy, even violent. Using tactics that shade into the next method, a manipulatrix gives her husband repeated discourses on trivial or nonexistent faults, shows brief looks of disappointment at any gifts (especially if they are exactly what she wanted or claimed she wanted), pretend that she has to realign the furniture and clean up every time he leaves a room, and acts unpredictably moody. The purpose is to tire him emotionally and physically while undermining his confidence, ultimately to lash out at and abandon her in despair. Contradictory behavior during especially stressful times can speed this process, as when a wife demands sex acts she refused in pretended disgust when he wanted them and claims he'd disappointed her when he "refused" to do them before.

Of the methods of suggestion, nagging and name calling are the simplest and most obvious forms. Juvenile as it appears, name calling is usually copied by others, bringing them at least subconsciously and in witnesses' opinions into sympathy with the manipulatrix. The names she calls a man are taken as an indictment of him unless they are stupid endearments intended to belittle and embarrass, and are believed as readily as copied. Name calling is especially useful when the victim has never done anything wrong.

In nagging the female constantly repeats what she wants a man to believe or do. Nagging plants ideas, usually negative and sometimes contradictory ones ("You're a slob," "You're too demanding," "You're inattentive," "You pester me all the time...") which are taken as positive messages about the woman. Nagging erodes the victim's stamina and confidence and can anger him without the female having to do anything overtly threatening. It burdens men with problems real and imaginary, indicts them for their supposed faults, and makes them feel guilty over things that cannot be atoned because they never happened. Since women nag about everything they are always able to say, "I told you so."

Nagging also supports two popular beliefs: as pleading that women are dependent on men, and as criticism that men are inferior beings requiring women to improve them. If a man resists nagging he seems at best unchivalrous and the woman persists in trying to "help" him, while if he gives in she's rewarded, continues him weak and contemptible, and so continues.

Suggestion takes many other forms. An aggressor tells her victim to do something she knows he's going to do --- or not to do something she knows he won't. This can turn an innocent deed into a multilevel conflict; the victim doesn't want to look or feel subservient, irresponsible, or stupid or let the manipulatrix think she's controlling him, but he doesn't want to neglect anything needing to be done, either, so he usually gets angry and sometimes confused, even self-doubting. Other times the female will scream or weep without apparent reason or speak in angry, demanding tones however bland her topic, all in order to infect the victim with, depending on his anxiety level, emotions the same as or opposite the one's she's feigning. Body language, already mentioned, can suggest emotion, contradict or reinforce whatever's said and done, get victims to imitate behavior in some useful context.

Common as it already is, male isolation is a secondary goal of women's manipulation. Men's work and aspirations as well as rivalry and chivalry isolate them. Their jobs frequently leave men exhausted and limit their recreational and other options, but most willingly take on such tasks because they want to build and provide for families. Chivalry, as we'll see later, is a powerful factor. In a gender conflict it leads people to side with women and redouble their attacks on men who try to defend themselves. To isolate a man a woman need but pretend to be frightened whenever he's around. Still other goals are to make him run off without any apparent reason or to push an unstable partner over the edge.

Actual applications are so personal and numerous they are hard to see. If a man always goes to the bathroom at certain times the manipulatrix, seeking to make him a failure, will interfere before a social engagement or job interview or final exam so he'll be at least uncomfortable. Sex habits are a popular tool and more fun to read about than digestive regularity. A wife may perform fellatio for years, declaring how much she enjoys it, then suddenly refuse, claiming with equal fervor that she'd always hated it and he forced her to do it. Or, as noted before, she may refuse any sexual variation from the start and till he's learned to live without it, then bitterly criticize her husband for his routine, monotonous sex (often describing enviously how a girlfriend's husband does precisely what she refused with the greatest vehemence to let him do). Many times after settling into a comfortable, secure routine, expressing how glad she is to be free of the hassles of courtship, a wife will demand romantic silliness and dating behavior on the basis of her "mysterious" female needs. The real purpose is to frustrate and degrade the husband so he'll either be angered or will act as she demands --- for which she will despise him.

A female who always precedes sex with a certain sequence of body language and preparations will perform the same routine while a man tries to study or watch his favorite show, frequently to deny any seductive intentions if he responds. Another common application is to talk about something he likes while a man does something else he likes; if he's building a model ship, she talks about football. On the other hand, she may pair his likes with his dislikes, deciding to express her feelings about soap opera characters or eyeliner when he feels amorous or needs to discuss paying for car repairs. Yet another gambit is to go about her regular activities with the abrupt movements and sharp breaths of someone about to fly into a rage, then act romantic or helpful once he's prepared himself for the fit. Under any simple circumstances there's a simple statement that always disrupts a man's life: "There's something we have to talk about."

How useful habit and routine can be becomes clear when we consider what women's reveal. Many if not most females act emotional, disorganized, scatterbrained, even incompetent. A woman who does so occasionally is usually trying to avoid certain tasks she dislikes, while one who only occasionally acts rational is either rewarding a man by now and then helping, or working at some matter of particular interest to her. The woman who's always dingy is almost always a parasite trying to make men take on all responsibility; careful attention will show her female gadgetry, her makeup and underwear, efficiently arranged and may well reveal her secret bank account and who her paramour is.

Another is the wife who takes an interest in finance after pretending indifference or incompetence, even taking complete control. She is laying the groundwork for divorce and, first, wants a full account of her husband's resources. Second, right before her legal assault she will buy a lot of luxuries, especially on credit, to take free goodies with her and saddle her husband with debts that will cripple his ability to get good legal help or recover.

Manipulation, in fact aggressiveness in general, is easier for women than for men because of special conditions. The oldest and most universal, the belief that women are deep, mysterious, inexplicably wise and powerful beings despite being helpless, irrational, even stupid is the source of most of these and is based on immemorial tradition and men's personal experiences and supported by female self-interest. Different cultures structure these elements differently, glorifying women's reproductive power or regarding females as needing tight control, and in ours an emphasis on their supposed mysteriousness is used to raise them to extremely high status.

Belief in their "mysteriousness" supports women's use of ambiguity and helps place them beyond responsibility and criticism. Emotional outbursts, whatever their purpose, are taken as demonstrating women's alleged irrationality and profundity. They can wear sexy clothes and act seductive, then not only claim they'd dressed for comfort or get upset if criticized or propositioned, but insult men for not doing either.

One of the most popular of all uses of this superstition is, appropriately, the appeal to occult beliefs. When women claim "intuition" has enabled them to anticipate another's actions or a particular turn of events they most often mean that their schemes are proceeding according to plan. They will insist that a house has poltergeists or the like, meaning that they don't always have time to straighten up after the other guy leaves or that they regularly go through their husband's stuff. Before the days of answer machines and caller ID women spoke of the strange behavior of telephones to cover their receiving messages via ring codes from someone told to hang up if a man answers.

Disinformation is another use. The last thing the majority of women want is for men to know their actual motives and feelings, so they rely on their phony mysteriousness and false superiority to elude men's efforts to meet their repeated demands to be understood. They may say nothing or give childish responses, but their most usual maneuver when a man gets close to understanding, as mentioned earlier, is to yell, "No, that's not what I mean! You just don't understand!" It is obvious women do this deliberately, consciously, and for this specific purpose. There's still no way to verify another's subjective experience, but documentary evidence of this exists in feminist writings.

For example, in the introduction to her critique of the Parisian psychoanalytical establishment, *The Weary Sons of Freud*, it is noted that University of Paris philosophy professor Catherine Clement was harshly criticized by fellow feminists for using logic and reason in her writings. Why? Because rational, logically consistent arguments carefully thought out and meticulously presented make it impossible for women to scream "No! No, that's not what we mean!" when men discuss women's issues. It's all there in black and white, translated into and commented upon in clear, grammatically correct, logically consistent English by one Ms. Nicole Ball.

Another special condition, more particularly American, is the elevation of women to the highest social and moral status. Despite, or maybe by means of changes in sexual attitudes we are in fact living out the culmination and fulfillment of victorianism rather than its defeat. Because of their status women are above criticism and objective comment and may be discussed, if at all, reverently, with repeated praise, and if for any reason negative observation is unavoidable it must be expressed through clichés and endless qualifications and circumlocutions and the fault ultimately laid to men. There is a cadre of feminists who with their pet wimps publicly bewail women's alleged poverty and lack of status, blaming Western civilization's "patriarchy" and "oppression of women" though we are actually almost the only civilization ever that does *not* practice these. The purpose is to preserve female status and power by using the power of suggestion through loud, repeated lies.

Every institution from law to media supports the doctrine of female superiority, so beyond disinformation uses it has widespread psychological effects. Women are rendered selfish, egotistical, and anti-social. Defined as crude, vile, worthless, lust driven brutes, men are indoctrinated to believe that only these callous semblances to femininity can redeem them, that they aren't complete or even real without women --- who don't need and are defiled by them. Socially, men must "prove" they aren't gay or impotent or pedophiles or rapists by appearing with and submitting to women; the man who shows up without a wife or date is suspect and in social, sometimes physical danger. Men who see women as their moral superiors don't judge their behavior or evaluate their characters or dare to think they can define females' motives, much less criticize them, and are in any event terrified of women's rejection.

Elevated status is also a courtship device. It aids women's mate selection by showing up which men are eager for it and which don't believe in it. It also helps lessen competition between women to the extent that being so far above men they all seem more equally appealing and that, depending on a man's character, their supposed ability to supply personal fulfillment becomes more important than their physical desirability. On the other hand, because men are taught they are nothing without women, another manipulable want is added to their motives and so their rivalry increased.

Built upon the above and other elements, the peculiar institution of chivalry is the most important of these special conditions because it permeates everything, is legally enforced, and gives women behavioral *carte blanche*. They don't necessarily have to obey the law, for example. However heinous her crime a woman will seldom pay more than a token penalty. If she must go to court she will usually have a show trial whose outcome is understood in advance; the authorities will likely accept her excuse, however ludicrous, and whenever possible blame a man. This means women are free to use any form of aggression and so husband murder for "years of abuse" is understandable as a way to avoid the possible loss of part of a man's property in divorce. It goes without saying that women are virtually guaranteed success in civil litigation and comes as no surprise that there are vast tax supported agencies that minister not only to their needs but to their demands.

Because of chivalry marriage isolates men and serves as an extortion tool against them. Most men willingly sacrifice friendships and kinships and interests to their new families and the work that supports them --- and are as savagely criticized when they do as when they don't. Men are pressured to give up everything and are put down for the effects this is supposed to have on their families while women, assumed family oriented in everything they do, keep female friends and stay close to families and are free to blame their husbands if they can't maintain their interests.

Legal favoritism of women turns marriage against men, making divorce an omnipresent threat. The husband always loses, whoever's usually to blame, losing at least half his property, control over future income and possibly his pension, often continuing to pay the female's bills and insurance, and always has to finance the debacle. He usually loses access to children and is relentlessly criticized because their mother keeps them from seeing him. Divorce, like marriage, costs women nothing.

A wife throws out her husband's comfortable old coat or shreds pictures of former girlfriends in order to assault his identity and anger him. If he complains, he's unchivalrous and in the wrong. She is understood to be improving his slovenly boorishness and jealous because she's hopelessly in love. We've seen that merely acting frightened or concerned causes others to "protect" women who do so. Feminists have turned chivalric behavior into a tool against decent, hard working, family oriented men who are hard to divorce by launching a general campaign preaching that all men are violent child abusing rapists then pushing through legislation against "wife rape," "violence against women," and the like. By chivalry women's words are accepted in court against all evidence, which is why this works.

Chivalry has subtler but no less pervasive effects. Most men will eagerly do for women things they can easily do for themselves and will almost as readily accept blame for women's deliberate wrongdoings. They will compete to wait on women. Politeness --- opening doors, helping women lift and carry, giving up seats to them --- has become a submissive gesture that women can, as members of the highest social category, ignore, demand, complain about, or revile men for doing or not doing.

Less noticeable because it doesn't at first appear chivalrous is men's sexual "obligation." Men are expected to make seemingly informal humorous overtures toward most of the women they see daily, even those who don't interest them or who are clearly unattainable. Not to flatter them with this submissive gesture can result in harassment by both sexes even though to do so can bring on lawsuits. On the other hand a man who refuses a woman's advances can be treated as badly not only by women but by men who'd nevertheless rage with envy and jealousy if he'd accommodated her. These routine gestures signal a man's submission and let women evaluate his pliability as their own status is reinforced. For their part, women signal that men are to behave chivalrously by pretending to be stupid, acting confused or silly, or acting frightened and vulnerable. In other words, by displaying certain signs of sexual receptivity.

Role ambiguity is a final condition. While their social and occupational options have expanded to include men's, women haven't suffered any equivalent losses as, for instance, being any more liable to be held responsible for their own actions. Women can blamelessly avoid unpleasant or unglamorous tasks by claiming weakness right after bragging about their ability to perform them. Women can claim to be excelling at traditionally masculine activities while following lower standards than men. They can demand chivalry after being insufferably rude and crass. In short, women can change roles at any time on the basis of situational expediency or even pure whim and pay no price.

Private relationships aren't easily grasped even though we all engage in them, partly because we do so semi-consciously and also because the exchanges they involve are transitory and particular as well as because nearly all persons protect their feelings. Manipulators evaluate and experiment with victims, tailoring their methods to individuals and altering them as needed. They use highly personal traits, objective self-knowledge being difficult and rare, and people who understand manipulation seldom discuss it. Successful aggressors are loved and admired, so describing their actual behavior has the effect of discussing beloved Old Masters' works as the smears and splotches of dried goo that they actually are.

Established science isn't very helpful since psychological lingo serves mainly to disguise practitioners' motives as it describes the effects of brain diseases, slanders persons shrinks or their employers dislike, and encourages self-indulgence in lieu of action. Nobody, least of all experts like politicians and salespersons, wants to acknowledge the power games in relationships, let alone reveal how they win them. As a power elite, women likewise discuss in code the use of people while denying it, protected by chivalry and status.

Many religious teachings are more objective and available, especially those designed to be understood through practice, but they are also often tied to specific cultural contexts and, alas, to ethnic and other conflicts. This is why I have tried to consider relationships and "social science" objectively and devise a terminology with which to understand and discuss the gender issues that are now such a dilemma. To see how women's natural self-interest has been perverted by feminists and certain authorities into a socially destructive egoism and to see this in our own lives is to be able to make the simplest available step toward a solution: solving our individual relationship problems.

How Women Manipulate was published originally by Textar Media, Inc. in booklet form. Copyright 1996 by David C. Morrow.

Notes on the Feminist Control of the Media

Ten years of writing about men's issues [as of 1986] have made it clear to me that the established media is controlled and manipulated by feminists. With rare exceptions both news and fiction, whether on television, in movies, books, or magazines and newspapers, conceal the truth about the male situation, particularly with regard to divorce, in order to further feminists' anti-family purposes.

A standard propaganda technique is to ignore truth, sometimes to present a lie as reality, and media feminists make full use of it. Truth is that men want family stability while women, who get child custody in 97% of cases, initiate most divorces, and that men are jailed for nonsupport although courts don't usually enforce visitation. In response, the men's movement, composed of groups from local to international size throughout Europe and America, has tried for decades to get justice for men and children.

Except for occasional local items and a nod now and then to "male feminists," the news media don't cover men's issues. They go overboard to accommodate women, they glamorize gays, they even report on grandparents' visitation rights, but of heterosexual family men they say nothing. As far as they are concerned the men's movement doesn't exist because they intend for the public to be ignorant of it.

This isn't true of the non-Western press. For example, two years ago *Asahi Shimbun*, Japan's leading newspaper, did a documentary on the men's movement. In October 1981 I met with their reporter, Mitsuko Shimomura, at the Dallas Fairmont and found her fully acquainted with men's issues and organizations as well as such leaders as Tom Williamson and John Rossler. So Japanese readers know more about the American men's movement, thanks to each country's media, than most Americans.

Outright censorship rather than simple omission is also practiced. Wisconsin activist Roy U. Schenk has presented his comprehensive theory of the male dilemma in a book entitled *The Other Side of the Coin, Causes and Consequences of Men's Oppression*. In the January/February 1984 issue of *Transitions* he writes that his book was banned by the Madison [Wisconsin]

Public Library, kept under lock and key at the University of Wisconsin, and "disappeared" from the local technical school. *The Capitol Times*, Madison's liberal newspaper, and a student paper called *The Daily Cardinal* heaped bitter vituperation upon Dr. Schenk and his book, while the latter was banned from a Minnesota feminist "men's" conference in October 1983.

The media also try to convey and reinforce feminists' essentially hateful image of men. Television comedies depict men as pompous buffoons and incompetents, especially Norman Lear's productions, which include "One Day at a Time," a long lived program glorifying a woman for running out on her husband and taking his daughters.

Seldom is the actual truth about divorce presented, however, since the purpose is to depict men as self-centered, lust-driven brutes. Divorce statistics are a matter of public record, making it comparatively simple to verify that most are sought by women and contested by their husbands. Nevertheless, the media usually depict men as leaving their families. Such hit movies as *The Exorcist* and *E. T.* present the husband's desertion as a fact of life, perhaps the ultimate cause of the dramatic conflict. *I Ought To Be In Pictures* depicts a daughter's quest for her runaway father.

Not that feminists would approve. Their objective is to bear children by a couple of husbands to hold for support and inheritance purposes. This creates two problems: getting rid of the father and denying the proven fact that most child abuse is committed by single mothers or, with their cooperation, by their boyfriends and subsequent husbands. One way of handling this is to use a few, comparatively rare instances of misconduct by natural fathers to smear them with their successors' vices, hence such incest horror stories as Louise Armstrong's *Kiss Daddy Goodnight* and *Father's Days* by Katherine Brady.

The true motives of feminists are nowhere more clearly revealed than in their response to questions asked by Collette Dowling, author of *The Cinderella Complex*, about their view of joint custody. They answered that it "would destroy our power base..." and that's just what publicity would do.

Thus we can see that men's efforts at divorce reform are identical with conservative groups' demand for legislation preserving the family and that feminists oppose both. Since men have such difficulty presenting their case through supposedly open such difficulty presenting their case through supposedly open and objective standard channels in America and Europe, it is clear that the Dan Rathers, The Norman Lears, along with their media and academic colleagues all down the line favor feminists and those with like goals. It is clear, too, that they are attempting to use their power to stealthily impose their anti-family collectivist revolution on a society that neither needs nor wants it.

"Notes on the Feminist Control of the Media" appeared in *Critique*, Volume VI, Number 1 and 2 [# 21 & 22], Spring/Summer, 1986.

What About Central Park?

For something that seems to prove men are the brutes feminists claim, the Central Park debacle [of 11 June 2000] has faded rather quickly from commentary. The news wouldn't give us the whole story anyway since that might clarify who was to blame.

How were the young women behaving prior to the scenes shown on the news? They'd likely also had too much booze and pot. Their outfits certainly appeared skimpy. Did some engage the men in saucy repartee, squeezing through the press of bodies and making risqué remarks? Did some flash the crowd making double entendres about being hot and needing to be squirted? If any did, the media will try to keep us from finding out.

This incident could've happened in 1950, with women acting that way, but it would also have been a very different incident. Since traditional mores are reality based, women brought up then knew they were autonomous persons responsible for their own behavior and knew how men saw their actions. Any of them who acted like their granddaughters do or even just plunged into a mob of strangers would've been trashy individuals who intended to be groped. Yet I doubt that's what their granddaughters in Central Park intended or even thought possible. Teasing men is an ego trip that today's girls have too unrealistic a concept of human nature to indulge. They are reared on feminist claims that they are stronger than men who, terrified of them, will either just stand there drooling or fight each other. They simply don't understand men. Normal men aren't afraid of anything except other men and have a natural inclination to protect women that our society cultivates. Apparently today's girls don't understand that self-control, including their own, is soluble in alcohol, either.

It's amazing that men usually do behave decently after decades of feminist venom. Men cause all the world's problems, they constantly "hurt women;" if they're polite they're cold and repressed, if not they are weak or violent. By turning men against each other feminists have extended the anti-male bigotry of divorce courts throughout society, rendering schools female institutions, burdening businesses --- businessmen, that is --- with political correctness, and turning the military into an experiment in female favoritism. The media continuously spew anti-male messages nobody would tolerate about women. Even men's restrooms, but not women's, are no longer private. Little wonder men might sometimes act out and that the male cops they'd normally fear, sick and tired of the same abuse, might sometimes just watch.

Pathological women have always misused male chivalry and protectiveness. A girl with two suitors, for example, tells each the other bothers and frightens her, then chooses the winner (or loser). A husband doesn't spend what his wife figures she's worth despite their poverty, so she tells her father or brother that he hits her. The dictum that the personal is political, feminists' basic strategy and only even halfway original idea, is the prescription for extending this neurotic maneuver. The same female charges her husband with abuse, knowing that no judge will ever question a woman's accusation or listen to a man's defense. Feminist lawyers define the most numerous and wealthiest population, women, as an "oppressed minority," turning every institution against men.

Though apparently supporting their misanthropy, Central Park actually worries feminists. The men acted according to nature rather than women's dictates or the manners feminists have done so much to destroy. Men aren't cowed and controlled, they resist abuse, and they don't automatically attack each other when women misbehave. Men are seeing through their manipulation and, like them, normal women are dangerously close to realizing feminists have dealt us all a pack of lies.

That's why, editing evidence and instructing us in what to see, the media made this local incident into a national issue. The intent was to foment a hate revival with people chanting feminist mantras like clones in an Orwellian hive, distracted from their insights, reabsorbed into the party line, drowning out anything else. The response I saw was people questioning the women's behavior and partly sympathizing with men who've endured decades of hate rhetoric. That's why the editorials stopped: they were raising consciousness of who was really to blame.

"What About Central Park?" Appeared in *Transitions*, Volume 21, Number 1, January/February 2001.

What to Call Crissy

In August '02 there was an exchange largely by NCFM e-mail concerned with finding the best term for a certain female type. Women who, wrote BMFB on 12 August, exaggerate silliness, sex appeal, and arrogance. These are the ultra girlies seen on television as Charo's stage persona, Pamela Anderson as Valerie Irons ("VIP"), and, most obnoxious of all, Crissy on "Three's Company," played by Suzanne Somers.

Among other manipulative and evasive behaviors, such women pretend to be stupid or weak whenever they feel too lazy or irresponsible to perform some task. By acting silly they signal men who are under social pressure or who are weak or naïve to act chivalrous. They may get these guys to attack a man they're mad at by acting as though frightened. They pretend to be "traditional" to avoid work and responsibility and "modern" when horny. When not totally indolent they radiate sex appeal or anger or both.

That this female type must be portrayed comically save in a couple of limited dramatic forms --- biblical epics, for example, and sometimes *film noir* --- points to the need for a term enabling us to discuss them directly and realistically.

Some possibilities were suggested in a thread called "Macha vs. Bimbo." *Macha*, created by analogy with the adopted Spanish word *macho*, supposedly means the latter's female equivalent. It doesn't appear in Velásquez' Spanish dictionary, which lists words overlapping the intended meaning. *Mujeriego* means womanly or pertaining to women, *mujeracha* a coarse woman, and a *mujercilla* is a hussy or strumpet. None are exactly right or anglicize well, and macha seems more amazonian that girlie.

Bimbo does suggest a dim brained party girl. Chapman's *Dictionary of American Slang* gives it as an Italian word for a baby that became a popular name for a monkey, then a term for a thug, and finally around 1920 for a female prostitute. It fails to convey the callous egoism that more often than stupidity underlies these women's behavior.

In an 18 August postal letter F. Baumli suggested *fluff*, Australian slang of a couple of decades past. My copy of Wilkes' Australian colloquialism dictionary doesn't list it, but Chapman gives its American meanings as a stupid superficial girl, a flubbed theatrical line, and empty rhetoric. It conveys superficiality very well but no suggestion of other traits.

A new word based on or suggesting Classical roots could carry the needed range of meaning and implication without such slang limitations as a narrow range of users and too close an identification with a particular era or fad. Examples are *gynoporn* for material appealing to women's prurient interests such as *Cosmo* type magazines, bodice rippers and other romance novels, and chick flicks, and *manipulatrix* for a purely manipulative female. Tom Goldich originated the idea in the bimbo-bitch case in an e-mail suggesting a word be built on the Latinate root *fem--*.

Adding to this the Latinate suffix *–issimo/a*, meaning "most high," "supreme," "ultimate," and the like and shortening the result for simplicity yields *femissa*. This literally means something along the line of "superlatively feminine" or "really girlie," with meaning and sound appropriate to its purpose.

Femissa carries the idea of exaggerated femininity and has the gravity to convey the malice festering inside all but a few such women. As a new word, it is a blank to be filled in. It echoes the English "sissy," "prissy," "missy," "miss," "misanthrope," even "abyss" and "mantis" among other words, yet its roots make it easily accessible to many non-English speakers. Femissa can be a noun or an adjective, maybe even a verb (perhaps *to femiss* or *femissate* or *femissolate*). Tom Goldich notes by e-mail that it was simple and conveyed the notion of an effete spoiled brat useless for work.

Example sentences come to mind. Crissy was the femissa roommate. The rich old guy married a femissa. That daughter of yours is becoming a regular femissa. The novel traces the development of an amoral femissa. That girl's a femissa; avoid her, son. The serial killer singled out femissas. Get her around men and she goes totally femissa. It's fun to watch her femissolate.

It seems like the right word to me.

"What to Call Crissy" has not appeared elsewhere.

The Perpetual Defiance Charade

The issue camouflaged in certain "womyn's herstory" constants became clear when I was reading *Taking the Wheel*, an account by Virginia Schraff of women's influence on early automobile development. It wasn't by the author's intent, but by my reaching a cognitive saturation point. No rabid man hater, Schraff does claim that women have been oppressed. She presents some well reasoned interpretations of verifiable facts. Yet like much of recent [2001] feminist writing it seemed her text could be cut by at least a third. Today feminists know better than to rely on vehemence and sheer fantasy. Typically, what's important is embedded in a web of apparent irrelevancies not unlike those that legally naïve witnesses include in police reports, punctuated by occasional absurdities. These authors know what they are doing and their fluff serves a purpose.

With a fine word picture of the middle class city woman circa 1890 going shopping, Schraff deftly illustrates women's role in creating a market for affordable personal cars. Her long skirts trail through horse droppings and garbage as, whatever the weather, she walks to where she can board a horse drawn or electric trolley. Packed in a crowd of often unwashed strangers, she's groped by men. She has to return home by the same means and must usually have her purchases delivered. Circumstance and motive made clear.

Following this objective, insightful introduction Schraff lapses into sexism over, of all things, power sources, and into the contradictions that comprise much extraneous material in feminist writing. She scarcely mentions steam cars or that it has taken more than a century to develop electrics approaching the practical usefulness of other types. Instead, she ridicules men for thinking women preferred the weaker electric cars and accuses them of macho posturing for preferring gasoline engines. Then she cites examples proving that most women preferred gasoline power. Society girls like Alice Roosevelt made long trips and daily headlines in gasoline cars. Race drivers like Claire Rochester and Joan Newton Cureo --- the latter famous for racing between 1905 and

1909 --- competed in them. Schraff tells us that many female ambulance drivers used them on World War I front lines.

She certainly does show that from the very beginning nobody could keep women from driving what, where, when they wanted. That's what we'd expect after Schraff showed how crucial they were in turning an experimental gadget into household equipment. Yet a recurrent theme here and elsewhere is that women "defied tradition" whenever they took the wheel. Such apparent contradictions are tacitly understood by feminists and their *apparatachick* as referring to realities they can no longer deny or distract people from by screaming. Like oxymorons, male bashing is now a convention of feminist writing as much as it is an expression of emotion.

This shows quite clearly when Schraff sort of admits women's role in developing electric starters. I've heard my grand-parents mention the difficulties of crank started engines as well as seeing examples in print and video media, so I can evaluate her comments. Schraff wants to give women credit without admitting that perhaps most of them weren't strong enough to crank up their cars and that even those who were had a cultivated manner of superiority and so tried to get men to do it. It may be her zeal to compensate by exalting women that caused her to overlook the obvious facts that many elderly and disabled persons couldn't start their cars, either.

Instead she presents hand cranked engines as dangerous (which they could be) and tries to imply that their long career was a ludicrous and unnecessary male preference ended by female common sense. One of her examples is a news item about a man who stopped to help a woman restart her car, suffered a broken jaw when the crank suddenly reversed, and in those pre-antibiotic days swiftly died of gangrene. She narrates this with typical femi-nist callousness, ignoring the chivalry and male willingness to sacrifice for women that she has probably often exploited to tacitly ridicule men. The reason is to disguise and draw attention from female weakness, real and pretended, that sped the development of electric starters.

I'm not doing a review of *Taking the Wheel* but a biopsy of a feminist literary convention. In accomplishing what they intended, showing women's profound effect on the course of events, feminist historians have shown something they did not want to or expect. The symptoms in this book are the strategic use of male bashing and the assertion that women who drove were "defying tradition" even though they'd been active in creating the situation. That they'd "defied tradition" driving in 1925 and would apparently be just as "defiant" driving in 1945 even though they'd already "defied tradition" by driving in 1900.

Reading this I recalled a TV documentary about female stock car racers in the 1940s and 1950s who were of course going against tradition. If their grandmothers' generation were race drivers before 1910, I wondered, exactly what tradition were these ladies defying? The real object of Schraff's study and obfuscations is that women didn't invent the automobile or any of its vital components, but simply realized how convenient it was and wanted it.

In one form or another this is the subject of recent feminist histories. By the late 1800s, according to Judith N. McArthur's *Creating the New Woman*, women had set up charities, social clubs, educational and reform organizations, and political lobbies on a national scale. She shows them to have been the major force behind legislated race segregation and admits that while men of different races mixed freely because of work and shared interests like sports, white women, who were happy to have black women do their chores, didn't want black men around. This carefully researched truth contradicts feminist assertions that women were powerless and that all women are always accepting and caring.

So McArthur makes the incredible claim that the appliances invented during the era she discusses --- refrigerators, sewing machines, washing machines, vacuum cleaners, *etc.* --- greatly increased women's housework load. Why, then, would anyone buy them? Behind this unsupported assertion lies the indisputable, verifiable fact that women a century ago wielded great political and social power and used it for ends now considered evil. There, too, lies the fact that the increasing leisure for women of all classes to become feminists is the results of men's inventions. Thus McArthur tries to show the "new woman" struggling against increasing drudgery when in reality rich, then middle class, then even many poor women enjoyed ever more freedom and autonomy --- which process was her subject.

In *Delinquent Daughters* Mary E. Odem shows women using their power to create the Progressive Era's anti-sex legislation (which feminists decades later denounced as "the Patriarchy's" attempt to control women's sexual expression). In studying that obsession with teenaged and young adult females' sexuality she illuminates another side of the behavior in question.

Certain fantasies emerge when women's power becomes obvious, reaching ever increasing hysteria as their power increases. In the era Odem studies these were most famously the "white slavery" panics that flourished between about 1880 and 1920. Most of us remember the "satanic abuse" and "recovered memories" hysterias that raged from the early 1970s through the 1990s when feminism was in full power. A clearly visible pattern of behavior that incorporates the prejudices of the day into a victimization scenario seeks to distract people from women's power and perpetuate the women as oppressed myth to absolve them from any responsibility for errors or unfortunate outcomes. Asians and Jews were kidnapping young white Christian girls and forcing them into prostitution. Those awful men are perverting and using innocent children, including their own...

In part it's the desire to avoid responsibility that underlies the tangents and elided logic of feminist histories, but there's also another purpose. When each succeeding feminist cohort rediscovers the bevies of female doctors, executives, lawyers, politicians, reporters, spies, whatever that fill the record they rage at the imagined suppression of women's accomplishments by male historians. "The Patriarchy," they shriek, has tried to consign women to historical oblivion.

Yet knowledge of females in history is available in any decent library. Roman women ran businesses, even construction firms. Medieval women filed lawsuits, made pilgrimages, established and ran businesses, attended universities, even strapped on armor and fought battles. Anne Bonney was a notorious pirate who operated off Virginia and the Carolinas. By now everyone knows Victoria Woodhull ran for president against General Grant. In 1900 paleontologist Dorothea Bates studied the interglacial fauna of Corsica and discovered several modern species as well. Men have no problem recording the deeds of women who play important roles (the very ones they should ignore, by feminist reckoning), of whom Cleopatra VII Ptolemy is a well known example. In fact, the record shows that save in Classical Greece, Western women have generally had social and political power and chosen their careers. Rather than men, it is usually feminists who come to the position of obscuring these facts so they can claim men did.

That's not only because the record shows feminists unnecessary but because it reveals another fact that kicks them in their fantasies. At least current gynorevisionists have quit imagining an amazon matriarchal golden age that those inferior men somehow overthrew. But why claim that women race drivers in 1950 had to "defy tradition" when they assert the same thing about those in 1900? Why claim that improvements in women's lives worsen their situation? Why is it "proof of oppression" that most women have chosen careers feminists despise?

What could be feminists' purpose in ignoring some things that make women look good? They once made a big deal of Rosie the Riveter but ignored the Confederate and Union women who worked in munitions plants and operated businesses while the men fought. They make little of pioneer women's strength and endurance except to claim it is ignored. Now that World War II is another generation past they seldom mention Rosie.

On the other hand, a couple of years or so ago some gender feminists declared that if higher education were sex segregated women would soon surpass men and be making discoveries men couldn't even understand. The majority of colleges *were* gender segregated through the nineteenth century and many remained so well into the twentieth and that didn't happen. It didn't happen in Classical Greece and it doesn't now or earlier in the Moslem world, either. These facts and the fact that earlier feminists demanded and achieved unisex classes the gender feminists either hadn't learned or conveniently overlooked.

Feminists practice situational scholarship, ignoring or emphasizing facts according to their feelings, for the same reason they cling to the myth of a vast immemorial male conspiracy working tirelessly to oppress women. Such nonsense allows each female generation to avoid personal responsibility and to "defy the Patriarchy" anew. That it glosses over or even ignores women's genuine influence and achievement doesn't matter to feminists. That it trivializes women doesn't bother them, either. All that matters is their desperate struggle against truth.

Like most women, most men fall into historical oblivion. They live their lives, tend to their families, practice their occupations, fight for tribe or country, perform their religious observances, and pass away to be forgotten utterly within a couple of generations. This is largely true even of rulers, whose names are recorded *ex officio* and of artists, whose works may endure for centuries. If you're not a historian you probably can't list the rulers of ancient Greece, the emperors of Rome, or the post-Revolution leaders of France, let alone the artists of the Italian Renaissance or the founders of modern physics.

However, you probably do recognize the names of Alexander the Great, Julius Caesar, and Napoleon, and not because they were men nor because they were generals. You probably know something about Leonardo da Vinci and Michaelangelo and even if you're not a scientist you've got some idea of Galileo's and Newton's and Einstein's work. Why? Not because they were men, but because they were *geniuses*. Their innovations are still used and their deeds still have repercussions and that's why they're in the history books. They'd be just as important and just as celebrated if they'd been women, and at least a couple of them were homosexuals.

It is the comparative scarcity of female geniuses that upsets feminists. I disagree with female novelist Taylor Caldwell who claims there are none. Marie Curie comes to mind along with Hypatia of Alexandria, who in late Roman times investigated the geometry of cones and cylinders. Maybe Elizabeth I and the poetess Sappho qualify. I would nominate the late Hedy Lamarr, who was not only a world famous actress but also spied against the Nazis and invented a radio controlled torpedo guidance system that's still in use. But nature seems to have so designed us that this fortuitous combination of intelligence, talent, and motive occurs most often in men.

Maybe feminists actually do believe that manipulating words is controlling reality. They use what they take to be clever tricks of reason and rhetoric trying to disguise facts from themselves as well as others. When they can't avoid facing up to Western women's exalted status, for example, they begin raving about women in medieval Japan and contemporary [1990s] Afghanistan. Similar is the rhetorical nonsense they issue when confronted with women's historical record in free Western societies: each generation is the first to rebel against "the Patriarchy," so achievement lies ahead. They will even repeat this about each generation in a long time span, even if to qualify it afterwards. Up to 1920 women were oppressed, but once they rebelled the world changed. Until 1940 women knuckled under to men, but after they defied tradition they were never the same. Before 1960 women were slaves, but then...

However otherwise excellent their scholarship, however well written their literary tantrums, however well planned their hysterias and self-repression, they are only fooling themselves and proving that feminists are far from being the smartest women around. And they are fooling themselves that the rest of the world doesn't see through it and isn't weary of their phony suffering.

"The Perpetual Defiance Charade" appeared in *Transitions*, Volume 22, Number 1, January/February 2002.

Who Are The Feminists?

Social roles need to be reciprocal. Strength and pregnancy determined traditional gender roles, which have usually used harsh penalties to force men to carry responsibilities --- family support, military service, civic duties --- compensated by financial control and occupational choice. Women, usually expected to be home-makers or entertainers, enjoyed high status, chivalry, and the right to shirk responsibility. Drastic circumstances and persons unable to live by the rules can alter practice, but to provide stability and security standards change more slowly and only when basic matters do.

The United States has changed dramatically as it arose with and nurtured the Industrial Revolution, grew swiftly to world power, and struggled to extend human rights. Gender roles have developed along with it to their present half-revised state. Advances in mechanics, then electronics have eliminated from most jobs the need for gross strength while medical science has brought reproduction under even greater control. Emergencies have to be met and jobs filled.

Truth contradicts feminist teachings, such as that World War II was a feminist watershed. America was. In the diary of midwife Martha Ballard, who died in 1812, we see that her contemporaries weren't surprised that she rode through heat and cold and crossed flooded and frozen rivers to reach her patients, was consulted by doctors, and ran her household. Frontier women loaded and fired guns and plowed fields while their urban sisters ran businesses and worked in factories. Confederate ladies ran plantations and worked in munitions plants. In 1872 Victoria Woodhull ran for president on a "free love" platform (the "sexual liberation" of 1972). By then Ballard's grand-niece, a doctor, administered a hospital staffed entirely by women. In the 1890s New York required state institutions to give female doctors hiring priority.

Even before women could vote organizations like the WCTU wielded enormous influence. Adventure was always "gender neutral," and the first female parachute jump was in 1913. An A&E film history documents that early 1900s movies showed women in heroic action roles, and Hollywood has always shown them as executives and community leaders. In reality, by 1925 women had with few exceptions acquired the same options and rights as men --- that is, nearly everything feminists now claim to be struggling for. Since social concepts lag behind practice, however, the formulae of traditional roles remain graven in attitudes and law.

Though they have complete freedom, women can still evade responsibility by acting stupid or weak. They can still expect chivalrous concessions and have such high status they can scarcely be discussed, much less criticized. Men, however, remain shackled to a narrow role of provider and protector, with no relief from responsibility. Only men can be drafted. Military women aren't expected to meet the same standards as men ("dual standards" is the term). Men are punished for sex with teenaged girls, women who abuse boys aren't [written in 1993]. Gary Dotson's case shows women can imprison men at random. Female criminals get lighter sentences and better treatment. Divorce judges, nearly always awarding maternal custody and jailing fathers unable to make payments, ignore their own visitation decrees. In this transitional era women have all the advantages.

So who are the feminists? Values are beginning to catch up. Sometimes women lose custody and pay alimony. Female criminals are more often punished. There's been talk of drafting women. Men are less likely to defer to them. The first of two answers is that feminists are spoiled neurotics terrified of having to outgrow their lives of irresponsibility and dependency. These reactionaries are trying to preserve gender inequality while pretending to fight it.

Since authorities naturally defend the status quo, outdated beliefs empower feminists. Conservatives indulge and cater to women because they consider them emotional and incompetent. Liberals because they consider them victims. Thus feminists need but look sexy and throw hysterical fits before senators, judges, and social workers. No democracy is involved in such feminist legislation as the slew of redundant measures like "violence against women" laws and "wife rape" laws intended to preserve women's elite status. Just as with the media, which blares their propaganda from every page and tube, feminists command and government obeys.

The feminist line is that evil, inferior men dominate good, superior women. Feminists use propaganda to excuse and glorify themselves and to foster hate. In the first case, women's successes are despite and their failures because of men. A girl advised against acting in porno movies screams that she will do it to defy "the Patriarchy's" plot to control her body. If she comes to grief, men made her go into the business, if she succeeds it's despite their efforts to stop her. When she gets too droopy to display, she earns money by denouncing the porno men "forced" her to make.

In the second, a girl sues the Boy Scouts for rejecting her membership application, claiming the Girl Scouts fail to offer what she wants. Logically, she'd benefit more from girls petitioning the latter to offer the desired activities. Logic is no more involved than in feminists insistence that all male but not all female clubs and schools are illegal, because education isn't the real purpose here; rather, it is to infect young minds with sexist hate through doing as well as teaching.

Their blatant hypocrisy reveals feminists' real motives. Some recently denounced birth control pills as a male invention designed to put reproductive responsibility on women, yet their perennial demand has been for complete female control of reproduction --- exactly what the pill provides. Certainly they'd have denounced a male pill as a plot to control women. The move to let women choose combat jobs is obviously a feint aimed at keeping military women from having to fight if they don't want to. Like abortion on demand, these things show feminists don't want adulthood. They want eternal adolescence, life by caprice and whim, with others (men, mainly) forced to deal with the consequences.

Amid claims they want financial independence, feminists push legislation adding ex-husbands' pensions to the divorce loot. They insist PMS doesn't disqualify women from strategic offices and that it so addles their brains it excuses murder. They claim women are stronger and smarter than men, who easily beat and rape them, and that they need separate schools to avoid masculine competition. The list is endless.

Most women, unlike feminists and the pathetic wretches who grovel before them, are honest hardworking individuals. Almost everyone, however, seizes opportunity when it arises and feminists have worked hard to convince women that serial divorce leads to prosperity via support and property settlements, plus inheritance possibilities, from several men. That's got to be why 80+ percent of divorces are filed by women, why the family is coming apart, why poverty is increasing, delinquency and crime are rampant, why people turn to drugs and fanaticism, why psychotherapists are rich.

Feminists, instead of working to achieve the balanced, equal roles necessary to our society's survival, are attacking its most fundamental unit. And that's why the second answer to our question is that they are the most dangerous, destructive persons alive.

"Who Are The Feminists?" appeared in *The Backlash!*, published by Shameless Men's Press, in August 1994. Copyright 1994 by David C. Morrow.

Toward Gynology

I was editor of *The Liberator* when, over a decade ago [circa 1980], I wrote a version of this article. It was to counter the so-called tender years doctrine and help men overcome the characteristic idealization of women that has always been the source of many problems that I began a column called "Life With Mother." There came an endless supply of items for it like the following which though adapted for the earlier version from *The Dallas Morning News* of the day are echoed in every newspaper before and since.

When a Mesquite, Texas divorcee moved her male stripper boyfriend in with her he murdered her young daughter --- upon which she promptly married him. Freed thereby from legal compulsion to testify against the man, she blandly stated that it had just been the little girl's "time to go." A Columbia, Missouri woman, already twice convicted of child abuse, let her live-in lover imprison her seven year old son in a basement for three months. In Carlton, Minnesota a divorcee joined her boyfriend in burning her two and four year old children. A divorced father in the Dallas suburb of Oak Cliff rescued his daughter, age twelve, from her mother and stepfather, who for over a year had subjected her to various sex acts with the forty year old man, pornographic photo sessions, and a spurious marriage to the stepfather to convince the child his behavior was legal.

Back then feminists were getting their anti-father child abuse rant accepted by authorities and the media, but there was always plenty of evidence that women and those of their sex partners not directly related to the children are the main abusers. Drawing upon reports of the American humane Association, the Association of Juvenile Courts, the National Center for the Prevention of Child Abuse, and the FBI's 1978 crime report, John Rossler of Equal Rights for Fathers of New York State estimated that mothers commit over two thirds of child abuse, 80% of it in sole custody and none in joint custody situations, while boyfriends and new husbands perpetrate most of the rest. A similar study conducted a few years earlier in Utah by Ken Pangborn showed abuse 37% higher among single mothers than the general population and that 67% of all abuse is the doing of women, of whom 80% are single mothers.

Emotional effects of maternal custody were also known. A 1980 study by the Charles F. Kettering Foundation and the National Association of Elementary School Principals reiterated what had long been common knowledge: problem children are primarily those from broken homes. There are diverse sources for the same fact. Over two-thirds of adolescents handled by the Florida Division of Youth Services that year hailed from broken homes --- which always means in maternal custody --- while R. F. Doyle found that University of Minnesota sociology professor Strake Hathaway, author of *Adolescent Personality and Behavior*, discovered that more than a third of children of divorce dropped out of school.

While gathering such information, Doyle discovered other facts. Professor Hathaway had calculated the delinquency rate for boys in maternal custody at 28.67% and for those with their fathers at 0.42%, and the ratios for girls at 18.19% and 0% respectively. As long ago as 1950, Doyle found, Harvard University's Eleanor and Sheldon Glueck showed in *Understanding Juvenile Delinquency* that children in the custody of mothers are three times as likely as those in fathers' custody to be troubled. Chinese-Americans, notes Doyle's associate, Professor Daniel Amneus of UCLA, comparing family structures in different cultures, "have until recently been among the most impoverished and discriminated against people in our society --- but they have the lowest crime rate because they have patriarchal families. Much the same is true of other Orientals, of Mormons, and of Jews."

Of course these facts and conclusions were censored by feminist controlled media and have remained so, being available to the few honest social scientists and those willing to do the research. However, even in 1982 there were opinions about the hidden truths. Some felt that fathers so seldom got custody (they admitted it!) that there's little basis for comparison; cited results, nevertheless, were corrected for numerical disparity, while cross cultural and historical studies supported them.

Some saw women's child abuse along with the rising crime and divorce rates as a symptom of social decline, others put these things down to "too much" freedom. Or they saw custody as especially stressful to women, though the same persons would raise a chorus of anti-male shrieks over the obviously valid recommendation for increased father custody. But there were other discoveries being made at the time that offered an explanation beyond further idealization of women. True, women were free to abuse because they were seldom held responsible for their behavior, much less punished for it, and feminists were working to eliminate even that, but there was emerging a clearer picture of why women abuse most and natural fathers least, and that immemorial laws existed to prevent such abuse.

In *Sociobiology*, E. O. Wilson considered a number of studies of infanticide, beginning with insects that eat their own offspring to conserve energy and control population, and continuing through fish and other lower vertebrates. Among studies of mammals, Kruuk reported that hyena pups may be devoured by adults in their pack, G. B. Schaller , whose study of Serengeti lions was published in 1972, discovered that a male who takes over another's pride may kill and eat his rival's kittens while the usually protective lionesses remain indifferent.

Primates are the same. Y. Sugiyama's 1967 study of Central Indian hanuman langurs, says Wilson, documents the slaughter of ousted males' offspring by successful rivals while females not only never try to save them, but instead immediately become sexually receptive. Anthropologist Sarah Blaffer Hrdy, author of *The Woman That Never Evolved* and a feminist despite disproving therein virtually every feminist fantasy, gives examples from higher primates, including Goodall's chimpanzees. Hrdy and Wilson suggested that it is advantageous to kill a rival's offspring, since neither the victor nor his new, now receptive mate will have to spend time and energy rearing another's descendants. Because of this the tendency to do so has been selected for during millions of years of primate evolution.

More such findings are published today [1993]. Not surprisingly, editors seem to have censored scientific studies unsupportive of the feminist belief system; it went against their politics to hear that chimpanzee tribes engaged in warfare and genocide, not to say child killing, while gorilla clans have a higher murder rate than New York City. Such atrocities are supposed by feminist theorists to have been invented by human males. Some "scientists" have ignored their own presented facts in favor of ideology, for instance admitted feminist Franz de Waal, who gave a telling revelation of the feminist mindset in *Chimpanzee Politics* where he recounted that chimps often kill and eat their own species' babies, carry out long and bloody vendettas, and beat up and abandon elderly kin and then suggested that they are better at interpersonal relationships than humans are!

Humans are the species carefully disregarded by scientists of unquestionable integrity who are fearful of objectivity about women, and who therefore refrain from rigorous study of them. Likewise, the media tolerates few editors who will accept anything violating the collectivist dogma that environment wholly determines behavior. Before returning to the evidence of primitive people that started this essay, we need some perspective on humans, though our scope must be limited. There are no surviving primitive peoples today, those with primitive technologies having had as much time as those with advanced ones to refine their minds and institutions. In the light of this, the most promising places to look for substantiating evidence is in certain enduring institutions, in legend, and in early history.

While human populations were once small enough for everyone in a group to be closely related and child killing equated with genocide, by the time writing appeared people were concerned with huge populations and politically important individuals. Still, everywhere basic stories tell of children cursed or abandoned, like Ishmael and the sons of Ham; of cannibal mothers and wicked stepparents. The slaughter of innocents, specifically to eliminate claimants to power, is a common motif from early times.

In ancient Ur, both literary and physical evidence show that as in many other countries a king's court, retainers, and family were killed and buried with him when he died, perhaps to avoid dangerous struggles over succession. When Europeans reached Baganda --- now part of Uganda --- they found a tribal practice whereby a new king inherited the harem of his predecessor (who was usually his father), then systematically killed the latter's relatives, who were usually his own siblings and cousins. An example of child killing after conquest exists in a familiar document which retains its eloquence after more than thirty centuries. In the King James translation of the Book of Numbers, Chapter 31, verses 9 to 19, it is related that

...the children if Israel took all the women of Midian captive, and their little ones, and took the spoil of their cattle, and all their flocks, and all their goods. And they burnt all their cities...And they took all the spoil, and all the prey, both of men and of beasts. And they brought the captives, and the prey, and the spoil unto Moses, and Eleazar the priest...And Moses said unto them, Have ye saved all these women alive? Behold, they caused the children of Israel...to commit trespass against the Lord...Now therefore kill every male among the little ones, and kill every woman that hath known man by lying with him. But all the woman children, that have not known a man by lying with him, keep alive for yourselves.

Though this tendency is probably wired into the human brain, as Hrdy and Wilson and now others imply, but dare not say, so is the ability to overcome habit and instinct. Wise men long ago must have seen that more cohesive tribes, then more powerful states could be built by ritualizing dynastic struggles and minimizing chances for strife among common folk. Practical wisdom, not "male chauvinism," created the child saving ideal of tribes with exogamous clans that decreed widows must marry their husbands' brothers. Similarly, Moslem tradition provides that a man who divorces a pregnant woman must take care of her, that a divorcee must be cared for by her own (and thus her children's) blood relatives, and that the father have custody of children aged seven and older. Upon such regulations great civilizations are constructed.

A large enough society has every kind of person and many problems that can bring it down. People who are unsophisticated, mentally deficient, neurotic, or criminal will abuse children despite rules. Men may mistreat their stepchildren because they see it as a way to punish defeated rivals (ex-husbands, ex-boyfriends) and vent their anger at being required to provide for children not their own. Women may commit child abuse for the same reasons as well as to minimize past affairs and prove present loyalty. If the pattern of harming infants in many other primate species extends to *Homo sapiens*, both men and women may engage in child abuse to sexually stimulate the mother. According to the degree of their own competence and for the reasons given above, the majority of people (who, under stable conditions are capable of repressing primitive urges) give tacit and usually nonverbal, often ambivalent messages to children that they are unwanted or unloved. When custom and law no longer maintain social order, the tendency to yield to primitive urges can affect the majority of people.

Our society is endangered by a breakdown of families caused by a delinquent legal system and by irresponsible antimasculinists. Divorce is highly profitable, and not only are the judges lawyers, but lawyers also comprise the largest professional block in most legislatures. Back in 1983 when I was working on this essay's earlier version, I wrote various state governments requesting statistics on their legislatures to be used in the anti-lawyer newspaper *The Truth*. Divorce reformer Norm Kopp had told me that the New York legislature was 20% lawyers. In Wisconsin, I found, eleven of thirty-nine senators were attorneys, and so were twelve of ninety-nine assembly persons, fifty-nine of whom called themselves "professional legislators." In Alabama seventeen of thirty-five senators and eleven of sixty-four representatives were barristers. And so on...Little can have changed since.

The effect of many laws is to bribe women to divorce with promises of life long support, property settlements, child custody, and inheritance windfalls while judges ignore their own orders in cases where women violate them, and refuse to uphold fathers' rights. So, to line their pockets and pad their already swollen bankbooks, lawyers deprive children of potential protections and invite many women to drag their kids through lifetime careers of serial marriage and transitory affairs, creating the child abuse epidemic antimasculinists pretend to deplore.

The hidden agenda of antimasculinists, which reinforces the aims of the legal profession, is to keep most women emotionally adolescent and dependent on the welfare state while pretending to do just the opposite. A generation of screaming that they need no male support, for example, has provided women more government handouts and awarded men's pensions to women. The matriarchal family enables women to live an adolescent sexual fantasy life, without regard for the larger consequences, least of all the welfare of children. The effect is to make all men rejected suitors, worthy only to pay; all children abortable or abusable, with the natural father being the number one antimasculinist villain because he is the child's best natural protection, and he is blamed for all problems. This trend portends the undoing of our society.

The more sinister motive of antimasculinist revisionism is to obscure the reasons *why* matriarchy is a disaster. Those who have described the roles of radical feminism and legal collusion in the dangerous social disorder have yet to finally disprove the worth of matriarchy. Men's advocates, political conservatives, and even the scientists who stop short of the irrefutable conclusion that there exists a semi-instinctive tendency to drive away (and sometimes kill) children in particular circumstances that most people are able to control by will or by following society's rules, even anti-feminist, even misogynist editors to whom the early version of this essay was sent --- none of them could deal with this issue.

If the instinctive resistance to discussing this topic were as strong as the primitive urge to infanticide we would only be able to study it indirectly in lower primates and would never have made straightforward prohibitions against child abuse. Wise men who lived before the time of Abraham knew about this subject and laid the foundations of civilization East and West when they designed the patriarchal family structure to minimize child killing and maximize human achievement. The leaders of many peoples in many times and places have done likewise. But current political inclinations seek to undo this.

Liberals have shown a propensity for antimasculinism, and Liberal ideas --- foremost of which is the belief that environment wholly determines behavior --- permeate our entire social order. A strong ulterior motive of the pathetic fallacy of Liberalism is to undermine individual confidence and convince people of the need to submit to totalitarian collectivism through the device of associating descriptions of innate biological differences with the rhetoric of racism, i.e. with similarly ridiculous stereotypes of all Jews as naturally greedy, all Africans as simple-minded, *etc*. This fabricated intellectual association has created a powerful academic and media taboo against the mere mention of the possibility of inborn behavior --- which denial contradicts, incidentally, the same pseudo-intellectuals groups' credo that all men are biologically predisposed to commit mischief and are intrinsically evil. At least Conservatives are unafraid to state that individuals can be born as individuals, with built-in temperaments and talents, and at least editors of men's rights publications are more likely to indulge or advocate Conservative views, and certainly very few Conservatives are unabashed antimasculinists.

Yet not only do people of both the Left and the Right refuse to accept or even tolerate objective discussion of women, they simultaneously insist women need special treatment. Liberals claim that as victims of millennia of oppression women need compensation. Conservatives explain that because they are weak, women need special privileges. Both camps insist that despite the obvious contradiction it entails, women are both superior to men and also equal to men. These inconsistencies are possible, and find a home in politics, because all such statements are rationalizations.

They are rationalizations to protect a value learned at mother's knee and reinforced on the playground, by every date and locker room discussion, in every encounter with custom and law, to protect it because it no longer has a useful purpose. That is the idealization of women as superior, delicate, spiritual beings whom men must serve, pamper, even worship. It doubtless protected and gave women social power during the Middle Ages, and in the form of upper class sex games gave the rising mercantile sector an elegant replacement for peasant mores. It also inspired the madonna/whore concept of women, and now that we can control reproduction and substitute machinery for muscle, it makes antimasculinism and matriarchy possible because it keeps women above meaningful criticism. It is now a dangerous habit of thought in need of being the final subject of the hopefully also moribund treatment of "deconstruction."

Objectivity, not hatred, is the opposite and the antidote of idealization. A decade ago men's rights workers who were bitterly critical of women rejected my effort at a scientific explanation of child abuse not simply because such ideas were academically taboo, but because their own anger at women was merely the reverse of adoration --- an updated madonna/whore dichotomy. They wouldn't even consider an objective evaluation of the issue, rejecting it angrily or arrogantly, because in being based on science it violated cherished myths and made them aware of their actual insignificance, which they could not admit.

The idealization of women, as it remains today, means that the only men capable of an honest appraisal of women are those who, to use the pulp fiction phrase, use their knowledge for evil purposes. Con men who go from one sexual conquest to another, perhaps abandoning unsupported children to their fates, or marrying repeatedly, skipping out with the wife's money sans divorce. Such men are the only ones to positively understand women, and will remain so as long as other men idealize females.

Despite its usefulness toward any end, objectivity is not an absence of human values. Those who try to see others objectively don't lay impossible expectations on them or abase themselves to avoid doing so. Objectivity is practical in human relations in the same way considering the human body analogous to a machine is a practical artifice: without that artificial attitude we'd still shake maracas over sick people instead of administering antibiotics or removing diseased tissue or setting bones. Now that a few men have overcome their conditioning as servants of women --- *and very many women are able to see men objectively* --- all that men need to do is be equally objective about women, and to create a gynology --- an objective science of women.

"Toward Gynology" appeared in *Aladdin's Window* Number 12. Copyright 1993 by David C. Morrow.